HOW TO WIN AT HORSE-RACING

"One of the best players I have known..."
Al Illich, Author of How to Pick Winners

" His selection method is by far the simplest and most sensible...{and} is logical...enough to fall well within the grasp of any player."
Tom Ainslee, Author of Ainslee's Complete Guide to Thoroughbred Racing

"This is a great, honest book with tons of information. The most important horseracing book in years!"
Whitney L. Cobb, The Basics of Winning Horseracing

"Very interesting reading for all race goers and is well worth the price. Far better than any system costing double..."
Philip's Racing Newsletter

D0967713

ABOUT THE AUTHOR

Robert V. Rowe, *Racing Action* columnist and former editor of *American Turf Monthly*, has written one of the best books ever on how to win at horseracing.

Robert V. Rowe is the real thing - acknowledged by all the greats in the field. His original research, including the most comprehensive survey of wagering trends ever undertaken, spans more than 50 years, and will show you, in easy to understand language, how to play and win at the track!

Here is his long awaited and definitive book - written in the easy-to-read and fun style his fans have come to expect over the years.

HOW TO WIN AT HORSE-RACING

Robert V. Rowe

Gambling Reasarch Institute

CARDOZA PUBLISHING

This book is dedicated to my two sons of whom I'm extremely proud.
In alphabetical order:
Ret. Police Lieutenant Michael Robert Rowe
Dr. Robert Kjell Rowe

Cardoza Publishing is the foremost gaming publisher in the world with a library of almost 100 up-to-date and easy-to-read books and strategies. These authoritative works are written by the top experts in their fields and with more than 5,000,000 books in print, represent the best-selling and most popular gaming books anywhere.

First Edition
First Printing   *March 1990*
Second Edition
First Printing   *March 1994*
Second Printing   *April 1998*

Library of Congress Catalog Card No: 93-74315
ISBN: 0-940685-45-0

Table of Contents

1. INTRODUCTION

Making money at the races takes skill and knowledge, and in this book I'll show you how to combine these important elements so that you can be a winner!

If you are going to view racing like most others do; if you are going to use the identical sources of information that most others use, and if you are going to approach handicapping from the same aspect as most others, you will lose like most others. You must have additional sources of information upon which you build your handicapping skills.

It is the objective of this book to show you how to handicap knowledgeably and sanely, and avoid falling into the trap of approaching racing from the same losing perspective that the public employs. The public per se loses about 20% on every dollar it bets. And - this is without considering the added percentage of losses incurred through betting the exotics and betting at OTB. Therefore, if you pursue the same course that the public does, you too must pay the same price.

The overall approach in what follows will be to first provide a broad view of what racing is all about. Then we'll narrow the perspective and concentrate on all the specific areas where an edge can be gained.

With that said, let's now get started on a journey wherein our ultimate destination will be the achieving of racing profits!

My Start in Horseracing

I started playing horses about 50 years ago, just about the time when the bookmakers, who operated New York's handbooks, were being displaced by the relatively new pari-mutuels machines.

My initial interest in racing was spurred by a basic fact. I had only an eighth-grade education, and instinctively felt that under such circumstance I might be at a disadvantage if I chose to be a doctor, lawyer or accountant. On the other hand, I didn't relish the thought of punching a time clock and working in a factory for the rest of my days. Somewhat desperately I sought to escape from what I perceived would be a life of drudgery.

When I discovered racing it impressed me as offering the panacea for all of my ills. It seemed the last stronghold of rugged individualism; an area of activity enabling anyone to go just as far as his or her personal ability would permit. One didn't require a doctorate, or have to cozy up to the boss in order to get ahead. That, in essence, was the lure with which racing beguiled me.

What I didn't understand at that time was that if someone possessed all of the necessary attributes that successful horse playing demanded, the chances were that those same virtues could carry him much further in practically any other field of endeavor.

Nonetheless, the decision was made. I'd study racing and become a horseplayer. Well, I've been studying racing and playing horses ever since. And, in one way or another have earned my living from this pursuit during most of my adult life; sometimes precariously and sometimes bountifully.

The Skill Factor

Good or bad luck in horseracing may prevail for a day or two, but at the end of any extended period of time the results achieved by the informed player will far outweigh the results of the player relying on luck.

On occasion, when I've tried to make this point to a casual race goer, the usual rejoinder has been to point out a horse that may have just gotten disqualified, or a favorite that may have broken down, and ask, "How can skill possibly control factors like this?"

INTRODUCTION

The answer is, "It can't." But, that's exactly where the short-range element of luck enters into racing. Regardless of how skilled one may be as a handicapper he still can never be certain about the outcome of a single event. There's no "cinch bets" in racing. On the other hand the good handicapper and knowledgeable horseplayer can know with near-certainty how his own, or any other group of selections will fare over a reasonable period of time.

Predicting Finishes

Despite racing's seemingly tenuous nature it is surprisingly predictable. One classic example is that year in and year out, at every circuit, from half-milers on up to The Big Apple, favorites will win about one third of all races, and successive choices will also win *exactly* their proportionate shares as well.

This may vary in the short term, that is, the second choices may win a disproportionate share of races for a week or so, but eventually this situation will balance out, and given time the overall percentages will adjust themselves. This business of fixed percentages hasn't varied in the last 50 years - ever since the advent of parimutuel betting.

These stable percentages apply to many other areas of racing as well, and they are what can provide the astute fan with a needed edge. We'll study these percentages in depth later on, but for now we trust the point has been made that racing is not a game of chance. It is a highly predictable pursuit, and the predictability is what makes it possible for the informed individual to be an overall winner.

Understanding the Game and Being a Winner

Unlike the Delphic oracle, I'll strive to provide unambiguous answers to questions that you as the reader may have in mind. Much of what will be presented will be based on a truly tremendous amount of statistical data which I've researched over a period of many years. Research has been my strong point inasmuch as I've had the incentive, time, opportunity and inclination to pursue it. I'll try to stick to whatever facts I've uncovered, and will avoid personal opinion and theory as much as possible.

However, it's vital for the reader to understand an all-important point: There's no magic formula that will prove to be the "open sesame" to racing riches.

There's no such thing as a mechanical system, or one single approach that will prove applicable to all races, or resolve all of handicapping's problems. Racing is extraordinarily complex. Each contest presents a unique problem. It's the player's own character, intelligence, analytical ability, self-control and degree of knowledge that, in the long haul, will dictate his chance of success or failure.

In the following pages I'll present whatever I believe to be valid based on personal experience. However, it will be up to you to either accept or reject the ideas and concepts offered. If they impress you as sensible, accept them. If not, simply disregard them.

Neither I nor anyone else can tell you how to handicap. In other words no one can tell you how to think or reason. The best that can be done is to provide the tools necessary for logical analysis which is the basis for fruitful handicapping. How these tools are used is entirely up to you.

Let's move on now and take our first steps toward winning at the track!

2. ESTABLISHING A GOAL

A good beginning for a study of this sort is to first establish our goal, and then define whatever problems there may be that could impede our attaining this goal. If this makes sense, let's get started.

The goal appears to be a simple one.

We seek to achieve success at the racetrack!

Success probably has different meanings to different people. Some might view success as simply possessing the knowledge and ability to hold one's own at the betting windows. Others could view it as having the capability to earn a living at the track. Still, a third group might readily settle for being able to eventually tab an elusive but worthwhile Pick Six.

For our purpose we'll define success as being the ability to - at the least - avoid losses. Obviously, once the player has attained this status he's only a step away from starting to show meaningful profits. So, if we're in agreement at this point, let's now see what the roadblocks are that confront us in our efforts to achieve this goal.

The facts are plain: Racing is one of the toughest gambling games to beat. This is so because of the extortionary tax bite taken out of every dollar that the public bets. In New York, and most other states there is a 17% tax on every dollar wagered in the win, place and show mutuel pools. Additionally, exotic bets, such as the Pick Six and Triple, are penalized at a 25% rate. Then, add to this something called **breakage** and approximately another 2% gets deducted. It thus becomes obvious that the public has about a 23% bite taken from every dollar wagered.

"What," you might well ask, "is breakage?" Most tracks break to the nearest dime. That is to say that if a mutuel payoff figures to be $4.88, the winning bettor will only receive a $4.80 payback. The track keeps the odd pennies. The rationale being that the pennies are too much trouble to bother with. This, despite the fact that long before the advent of helpful computers and hi-tech software, New England tracks were paying to the penny and having no problems.

But, as difficult as this may be to believe, it still isn't the end of the tax burden that the patron of this "Sport of Kings" is expected to uncomplainingly bear. Fans who patronize OTB establishments have (at least in New York) an additional 5% deducted from their payoffs.

If the track payoff is $6.20, the OTB deducts 5% or 31 cents additional from this sum, leaving only a theoretical $5.99 to be paid out. However, we again run into breakage so the OTB payoff now shrinks to $5.80. Is it any wonder that this is a tough game to beat?

Yet withal, horseracing offers a much greater winning potential than the average mechanical casino game that takes a far lesser bite out of the gambling dollar.

Roulette provides a good example. Even in Monte Carlo which takes only a 1.35% house cut, it is physically impossible for a long-term player to beat the game. Why? Simply because one is dealing with a l00% mechanical operation that is devoid of the human element, and there is no way to surmount its inexorable grind. This, despite the frequent tales that crop up about the college student or the accountant who has contrived a winning "system."

Anyone who bucks a purely mechanical game with a fixed deduction from each play must, over a period of time, wind up a loser.

Why is racing different? A good question.

It is different because you are not playing against the house. You are playing against your fellow fan who is subject to many human flaws that include misconceptions, biases and a general lack of knowledge.

Any profits which may be forthcoming must come from his

pockets and not from the track itself.

This is the encouraging aspect of racing inasmuch as there is no other field of commercial endeavor wherein the competition is so mediocre. This is not stated disparagingly. It is simple fact. The average racegoer who represents your competition, is neither well-informed nor a serious race player.

He is a butcher, a baker or candlestick maker who's at the races for a day of fun and gambling. He probably buys several "tip sheets" on his way in to the track; spends time at the $50 window to see who the heavy hitters are betting, and in the interim keeps busy seeking "information."

He and the type fan he represents makes it possible for YOU, as an informed player, to win!

3. HOW THE PARI-MUTUEL POOL WORKS

As stated, you cannot glean profits from the track itself. It must come from the pockets of other players. The track takes its cut before the running of each race and has little concern with who or which horse wins.

The only added benefit that accrues to the track after a race is run is when a low-priced horse wins as opposed to a longshot. Low-priced winners such as favorites imply that a greater number of $2.00 units were sold thus producing a greater number of divisions within the **parimutuel pool** (which computes pay-offs on the basis of $2.00 units). In turn, this greater number leads to more breakage which in turn benefits the track.

Example Of How A Mutuel Pool Is Split

Assume there's $100.00 in the pool. The track initially deducts 17% for its **take**. This leaves $83.00 to be divided among the winners. If Horse A, the favorite, has $40.00 bet on it, it means that there will be $43.00 in winnings to be split among the players who bet the original $40.00.

In theory the mutuel payout should then be $4.15 ($2.15 added to each $2.00 that the winners wagered). However, as noted, the track pays to the nearest dime on a $1.00 basis, meaning that the actual payout is reduced to $4.00. The track keeps an extra 3.75% in **breakage**.

Now, if a longshot wins, the track's little racket is not quite as lucrative. Example: Horse B, with only $4.00 wagered on him,wins. Using the same pool totals for illustration, the payout should then be $39.50 to $2.00 producing a $41.50 mutuel. The actual ticket though will pay only $41.40 because the track keeps the odd 10 cents. Reduced to percentages, this means the track benefitted by only 0.24% in breakage contrasted to the 3.75% it kept when the favorite won.

It's of minor interest to note that the losers reap a somewhat dubious advantage from all of this. The reason being that it's the winners who are obliged to bear the heavy burden imposed by the track's *take and breakage*. It's their money being taxed. The losers have already lost.

So, getting back to our premise: Hopefully we are in agreement that racing is a tough game to beat. In fact it is one of the toughest. However, unlike many gambling games IT CAN BE BEATEN! But, for these hoped for profits to become a reality it follows that for you to win more you must know more.

You MUST learn and know more than your neighbor if you are serious about improving your profit potential. The problem is as simple as that.

Also, the insurmountable fact is that before you can realistically think of producing a profit you first must get back $1.20 for every dollar you wager. In other words, just to break even you have to win 20%. Then, after this point, you begin to show spendable profits.

Our goal is to help you achieve this pinnacle.

To some the foregoing may seem somewhat forbidding, but if you go into this game with your eyes closed, or with a misconception of what the true picture is, you have little chance to succeed. On the other hand, if you know what you're up against, if you know the enemy, your chance of success increases appreciably.

There's still another factor worthy of consideration. Contrary to popular concept, the individual capable of producing steady profits from racing must by definition be a person of strong character.

Racing demands self-control, intelligence and a willingness to apply oneself. The weak-willed and the slothful can't survive.

Are you among the few who can succeed?

4. THE WIN, PLACE AND SHOW POOLS

You can beat a race but not the races.

This cliche has been parroted over and over without end, usually by self-appointed experts who know little about thoroughbred racing. Apparently the point being made is that on occasion one can get lucky and cash a bet, but overall a player must lose. It's true, the public must lose, but the basic premise that overall *everyone* must lose is without foundation.

Many times I've noted that when non-horseplaying acquaintances discover I'm "a horseplayer" they'll smirk and then sagely state something to the effect, "You know you can't beat the races."

My usual rejoinder, if I bother to respond at all, is to ask how they earn their living. If they tell me, for example, that they are dentists, I next ask whether or not they'd consider it presumptuous on my part if I made all-inclusive pronouncements about their profession when I know nothing about the technicalities involved. "Of course," such an acquaintance might answer, "but what I said about racing is simply a well-known fact."

Well, the following is tendered as merely one example that refutes this misconception that passes for public knowledge. However, the "system" is not recommended as being THE approach to winning at the races. It is offered merely as proof that one can win, and that there is such a thing as a winning "system."

The Tote Board

Every major racetrack has an infield **tote board** that shows the individual amounts bet on each horse in each of three wagering pools; win, place and show. Our current discussion will consider the relationship that exists among these pools.

In the previous chapter we discussed the mechanics of how a parimutuel set-up operates. Let us now see how the individual win, place and show pools function relative to each other. It should be understood that in each instance they are independent units.

That is to say the win pool is one complete unit. The place pool is another, and the show pool still another. Yet, despite this they share common ground.

Win, Place and Show Pool

The **top choice** (the favorite) in the win pool usually is (and should be) the favorite in the place and show pools as well. The second choice in the win pool will usually hold the same rank in the other two pools, and a similar relationship usually applies to all other choices right on down the line, whether we're dealing with a 5-horse field of entries or a l4-horse field.

At this point it might be helpful to clarify what a favorite is. As obvious as the term appears to be we note that many casual racegoers seem to be the victims of semantic confusion. It is not uncommon to hear a comment such as, "Both favorites are being bet," or "I can't make up my mind which favorite to play."

The fact is that each race can, by definition, have only one favorite. The **favorite** is the horse which at post-time has the greatest amount bet on it in the win pool. Even if Horse A has $100,001 wagered on it, and Horse B has $100,000, Horse A is the favorite and Horse B is the **second choice**.

Well, I'm glad we cleared that up.

Now, back to our discussion of betting pools. As implied in the foregoing, even without the approximate odds being shown, one could tell, by glancing at the individual totals in the win pool, what the order was of the public's choices, that the first choice would have the greatest portion of the total. The second choice would have the next largest amount and so on.

Also, if the electronic system of the win pool should suddenly malfunction and the board became dark, it should still be possible to determine the order of the various choices by looking at the distribution of the money in either the place or show pool. Logically, each choice in the win pool should have the same rank as in the other two pools.

Example: If a horse rates 40% of the win pool it should also rate 40% of the play in the other two pools. With only minor variations, and generally speaking, the percentages for all choices should be approximately the same across-the-board.

This then is how the mutuel pool system of wagering should work. In fact it is how the set-up normally does function. Nonetheless, the fact is that several times a day abnormalities may occur.

Playing Overlays to Win

An alert punter will be able to spot a horse that's substantially out-of-line in either the place or show pool as compared to the win pool. Looking for such spots and playing them consistently is a positive approach to beating the races.

Why is this so? You'll recall the statement that, disregarding exotic bets, the player is confronted with about a 19% **nut** that must be cracked before he can anticipate pocketing winnings. This being so, it then follows that if pool discrepancies of more than 19% can be found and taken advantage of, the player must then be an overall winner.

He would win to the same extent that the bets chosen were underbet, or - in track terminology - were **overlaid**.

The win pool, as opposed to the place or show pool, offers the truest criterion for judging what a horse's odds should be. Many studies, including one of my own that encompassed more than 10,000 races, have shown that horses, as a group, tend to win in direct ratio to the odds quoted against them.

That is to say that horses at 2/1 will win with greater frequency than those quoted at 3/1. Those held at 3/1 will win more often than those at 7/2, and so on down the line.

This being so, it indicates that the win pool is a valid criterion for gauging winning chances. Therefore, whenever pools are out of sync it must be assumed that it is **the place and show pools that are wrong** and not the win pool.

Let's look at an example of an out-of-line place pool:

Out-of-Line Example

We'll assume that the win pool shows a total of $1,000 wagered. Five hundred dollars of this is bet on Horse A and equals 50% of the total pool. We arrive at the figure of 50% by dividing 500 by 1000.

Glancing at the place pool we note that the total bet is $800.00 of which only $200.00 is bet on Horse A. If we mentally divide 200 by 800 we arrive at the figure of .25 or 25%. The difference between 50% and 25% amounts to a 100% variance, inasmuch as 50 is double the size of 25. This means that the player who bet on Horse A to place would be getting the benefit of a 100% overlay.

Notice that it wasn't necessary to make allowance for the 19% take and breakage. This is so because we were not trying to compute what the actual payoff would be. We were merely comparing total amounts bet.

However, to clarify our point, let's reduce the two amounts involved to theoretical payoffs. The win pool (after deducting approximately 20%) offers odds of 3/5 (a mutuel payoff to a $2.00 unit would be $3.20) because $500.00 has been bet on A, and there will be only $300.00 remaining as potential winnings.

In the case of the place pool bet (assuming falsely that the odds are arrived at in similar manner to that of the win pool), the odds, in contrast, would be 2.20 to one, or a mutuel of $6.40 for every $2.00 wagered.

In actuality the place pool payoff would not be this amount because the pool must be divided among two horses as opposed to the win pool that pays off only one horse.

We present the above figures only to enable you to make a theoretical odds comparison.

In order to compute the *actual* payoff for Horse A in the place pool we would have to know the amount bet on the horse that will share the pool with Horse A.

Example: There's $800.00 total available to be paid out after allowing for the track's bite. Horse C has $250.00 of this wagered on it. Horse D who runs in with C has $150.00 total bet. We therefore must deduct the total sum wagered on the two horses ($400.00) and we find that there is $400.00 of winnings left to be shared on a fifty-fifty basis.

Horse C's backers will have to split their half of the winnings ($200.00) into 250 parts which means that each $2.00 place ticket will have winnings of $1.60 (after breakage) and therefore gets back $3.60, whereas the $2.00 units bet on horse D will produce a $4.60 payoff ($200.00 in winnings divided among the seventy-five $2.00 bets made on Horse B.)

Simplifying Overlays

For those readers who don't relish arithmetic it might be reassuring to know that you don't have to do all of this figuring in order to take advantage of the type overlay we're discussing.

All that is really required is that you understand how to determine if an overlay in the place pool actually exists.

Let's look again at Horse A's win and place pool figures. This may serve to simplify the matter.

Horse A monopolizes half of the win pool total and 25% of the place pool total. As stated, this is equal to a l00% overlay in the place pool because, percentage-wise, there is only half the amount bet on the place end as there is in the win slot.

Now, if we have to overcome a 20% tax in order to emerge as overall winners it follows that by repeatedly getting 100% overlays we not only succeed in overcoming the 20% handicap but benefit by the surplus 80%. This 80%, in the long haul, would then approximate our winnings if we assume we wagered the same amount each time.

Of course this is an extreme example dramatized to make a point, but frequently one can find 25% to 35% overlays in the place pool. And, even if one were to average only 35% on such overlays it means he would have to be a long-term winner of 16% for every dollar wagered!

And - this frequently can be compounded several times a day!

Nonetheless, the major reason for not recommending this approach more highly is that it almost certainly requires the co-operation of two individuals; one to hold a spot on the betting line, and the other to keep an eye on last-minute fluctuations in pool totals. The trend for serious money to come in just prior to post-time makes this necessary.

Therefore, last-minute odds changes can influence the success or failure of this method. This could be a reasonable approach for a well-heeled bettor, but I doubt that it holds much appeal for the average fan.

Consequently, and trusting we made our point, let's now discuss matters of greater interest.

5. AN INSIDERS PERSPECTIVE OF RACING

Many players have a distorted viewpoint of racing. They fail to appreciate the fact that horsemen are in a business, and a tough business at best. The business consists of constantly striving to win enough in purse monies to cover their overhead and provide a livelihood. Failing to do this, they usually go out of business.

If they own and train horses for themselves, as a number of horsemen do, they obviously are responsible for their own attendant costs such as paying for stable help, feed tabs, exercise riders, shoeing, van shipments, and veterinarian bills. If they work for someone else, or operate a public stable, involving several different owners, they have the option of either producing or losing the patronage of their sponsors.

Keep in mind that the winning of a purse or any part thereof involves no additional financial risk on the part of the owner or trainer. On the other hand, finagling to cash a big bet - regardless of the confidence with which one might be made - still involves an element of risk. And, racing being what it is, the element is always a high one.

Many feel that trainers and jockeys generally are engaged in one huge conspiracy, and that betting coups are successfully executed in just about every race. This is far from the truth. I have the privilege of knowing a number of trainers; some as mere acquaintances and others I classify as friends. Far from being conspirators or working within an organized ring, they invariably are loners; close-mouthed about whatever intentions

24

they have, and most certainly not inclined to confide in other horsemen. A few owners are relatively big bettors, but I know of no trainers to whom this applies.

On the other hand, some trainers do have a following of *cloak and suitors* who are willing to send it in whenever the trainer gives the word. There's nothing crooked about this. In fact the astute bettor is helped if he's keen enough to observe such "abnormal" action taking place in the mutuel pools. But, even when such action occurs the hoped-for coup frequently fails. One reason is that in most races there will be more than one stable intending to score.

One of my clubhouse acquaintances does well with a little gimmick that seems to be his alone. He knows every New York trainer by sight. He also is aware that most of them continue wearing their morning work clothes in the afternoon. That is, unless they anticipate having their picture taken in the winner's circle.

On these occasions they usually dress up in their "Sunday best." Of course this player gets fooled frequently. Either the win doesn't come off, or the trainer who he's spotted might simply be playing host to a sponsor or friend. However, it's not a bad angle.

In line with the foregoing: One day at Belmont, prior to the first race, I was having lunch in the track's kitchen. As I was about to leave "Doc," a trainer, asked me to give him a lift to the clubhouse which is about a half-mile walk.

On the way he requested that I stop a minute at his barn. The minute turned out to be more like 10 and I was getting nervous that I'd miss the first race. However, Doc eventually appeared. He was freshly shaved and wearing his Sunday best. He looked like the caterpillar that had metamorphised into a butterfly. I knew something was up, but attribute my continuing friendly relationship with many horsemen, in part, to the fact I never ask for, nor do I even want to hear "tips."

Occasionally information will be volunteered. But, I rarely heed it unless my own judgement of a race is simply being confirmed. I've discovered, over the years, that horsemen, generally, are not very good handicappers! I attribute this to the fact that they, like a proud parent, seem burdened with a bias that leads them to over-estimate whatever horse is in their care. The best tips that I've received have been those of a negative nature advising me that a certain horse for one reason or another was not up to its best race.

This is information I listen to and it has saved me considerable money.

But, back to Doc; sure enough I checked the program to see if he had a horse entered. He did, in the second race, and the program's morning line rated it at 10/1. Checking the *Racing Form's* past performance records I could see the horse as a possibility, but not one that I'd care to bet. I decided to pass the race. Doc's horse won and paid a hefty $28.60 mutuel. Like I said, sometimes horsemen are right, but more often they're wrong.

The point is that racing is a business, and not a conspiracy. Each participant is out to get what he can, when he can and basically the game amounts to the survival of the fittest. Some horsemen, of course, are more fit than others.

All too often when a race is over I'll hear some loser who dropped a $2.00 bet scream words to the effect that Jockey So-And-So should drop dead, or that the horse involved should break a leg.

Even from somewhat less opprobrious comments made by the more intelligent fan, one has to arrive at the conclusion that the average race player must find solace in blaming his poor handicapping on an outside source rather than recognizing that it was he and his analysis that was wrong. A bettor can learn far more about racing and handicapping if he concentrates on his own weaknesses rather than trying to blame others for his failures.

When one views thoroughbred racing objectively it becomes a source of surprise that so many fans have a misconception about the degree of crookedness or skulduggery that exists. Undoubtedly racing, like any large enterprise that deals with money, attracts its share of unsavory characters, but fortu-

nately they don't last long. They may get away with their she-
nanigans for a time, but eventually they get weeded out.

On the whole, racing is at least as honest and probably more
so than most other sports and businesses. Racing is so competitive that the collusion or cooperation usually necessary for
fixing races is extremely difficult to attain. An average field of
thoroughbreds consists of nine horses.

This means that a would-be fixer not only has to cope with
nine often-unpredictable animals, but has nine riders, nine trainers and nine owners also involved in varying degrees.

It would be difficult enough to create cooperation or to coor-
dinate a group of three much less one composed of thirty six.

Furthermore, due to being in partnership with the State, racing is supervised and documented to a far greater degree than
any other sport. Every aspect of it is monitored and recorded,
from the money that goes into the mutuel pools right on through
to the running of every race. Under the watchful eyes of the
camera, State inspectors, the racing stewards, fans and even
fellow horsemen it becomes difficult at best for crooks to succeed.

A jockey at a major circuit would have to be clever indeed to
get away, for example, with deliberately pulling a horse or using a hand-held battery to encourage increased effort from his
mount.

However, no one suggests that these and other nefarious
activities are not attempted, and no one suggests that occasionally they don't succeed, but on the whole racing is conducted on a more than reasonably honest plane.

Another consideration, and a very important one, that helps
to rule out widespread collusion, is the fact that for jockeys,
trainers, and horsemen, racing is in most cases their life's work.
They can no more afford to risk their reputations, or leave
themselves open to blackmail by being part of a crooked
scheme, than a lawyer, or doctor could.

The shady business that does go on is usually performed by
an individual rather than a group acting in concert, and - as
suggested - such individuals eventually get caught and weeded

out. One reason contributing to this is the pressure that fellow horsemen exert on officials to do something.

If horsemen suspect another of crookedness (such as using a drug) they're resentful. Not necessarily due to moral indignation, but because money quite literally is being stolen from them.

Any trainer who enjoys an unlawful advantage is effectively depriving others of their fair chance to win purse money and earn their livelihood.

Still another factor that helps keep racing honest is the tremendous competitiveness and resentments that the game, by its very nature, arouses. Far from creating an atmosphere where collusion and cooperation thrive, exactly the opposite prevails.

Consider an everyday situation such as this; Trainer A spends weeks or even months babying one of his charges, trying to ready it for a winning effort. Prior to the big day he enters him in a final conditioning race and along comes Trainer B who halters the horse, reaps the benefit of A's efforts, and wins with it next time out Hardly a situation to generate good-will.

Or, Trainer C decides he's been running one of his charges over its head. He persuades the owner to let him drop the horse down from $35,000 into a $25,000 claimer. He fails to win that race and loses the horse beside, via the claiming route. The new trainer raises the animal in price next time out, and not only wins once, but continues thereafter to win several other substantial purses.

Obviously this reflects on Trainer C and makes him look bad. It's hard to imagine that he'd have kindly feelings toward the individual who created this situation, particularly if he was convinced that the individual had unfairly improved the horse via administering some form of drug.

This competitiveness and the often accompanying resentment carries over occasionally to jockeys and owners as well. Bear in mind that probably half of all races result in photo finishes. Losing a photo by a nose and thereby forfeiting the winner's 60% share of a purse to someone else is not a situation conducive to generating good will, particularly if one has not been winning many recent races.

In line with this thought, the following presents a personal viewpoint that some bettors might choose to consider. Whenever I've blown a bet on a close finish I tend to seek solace in the thought, "Hell, I've only lost $20.00. Imagine how the owner, trainer and jockey must feel who've missed out on many thousands of dollars."

Assume, for example, a race with a $100,000 gross purse. The winner's share would be $60,000 as opposed to only $22,000 for a second place finish. The winning jockey usually gets 10% for winning a major purse, and his agent usually receives 25% of this sum.

So, you can see that a lot of people, aside from the bettor, also get burdened with their share of disappointments.

6. THE MORNING LINE

The ***morning line*** is offered on every track's program for every race. It is intended to be used as a guide showing how it is anticipated that the public will wager. In other words it endeavors to predict what the final odds will be. It is not intended to be a handicap of the race or races.

More accurately, it attempts to handicap the public's betting habits rather than to handicap the horses themselves. See illustration below:

Eighth Race	Morning Line
1. Tobascus	2-1
2. Einstein Plus	9-5
3. J. Paul	4-1
4. Dreamy Jes	7-2
5. Bold Rocket	6-1

Yet, many fans have a misconception of what the morning line is and tend to place undue emphasis on it. They fail to realize that this line is merely one man's opinion (or sometimes that of two people working in unison). The accuracy of the line is totally dependent on the individual's skill, which in some cases is of a high order, and in others is very poor indeed.

One thing to bear in mind is that the individual who makes up the line works for the racetrack. In consequence it would not be to his advantage to discourage betting as he well could do. For example, if he knows that a horse should be 50/l or higher he can't afford usually to indicate this because the high tentative odds would tend to discourage play. The chances are that he would list the horse as a 20/1 shot.

In the same sense, if an animal figures so well that it looms to be 2/5 in the final betting, the line maker probably would indicate it to be even money (1/1). Again, the reasoning would be that this would suggest a more competitive race, and encourage betting as opposed to discouraging it by suggesting that there was a low-priced "surething" involved.

Most line makers tend to create a price line that totals 120% or more. This figure takes into account the track's take and breakage. This means that the line used allows for the track to take in about $123.00 for every $100.00 it pays out.

For example here is a morning line from an actual race, along with accompanying equivalent percentage figures. In this case the "book" came to a bit more than 23%.

9/5	35.71%
2/1	33.33%
7/2	22.22%
4/1	20.00%
6/1	14.29%
Total 125.55%	

The actual closing odds in this race were:

9/5	35.71%
9/5	35.71%
2/1	33.33%
6/1	14.29%
13/1	7.14%
Total 126.18%	

The final odds shown above (and on the tote board at the track) are merely approximations. In most instances the effective payoffs are greater which would tend to lower the total indicated.

Example: The horse listed above at 6/1 was actually $6.20 to one. This means that for every dollar wagered the player who bet the 6/1 shot would get back $14.40 for each dollar wagered and not just $14.00 if he won.

Note that payoffs are usually stated as being TO $1.00 and not FOR $1.00. The difference is that in the first instance an 8/1 horse would pay a minimum of $9.00 whereas in the second example he'd return only $8.00 for a $1.00 wager.

People attending the track for the first time frequently confuse the terms when trying to compute possible winnings.

The Dutch Book

The same type of line that guides the track's morning-line maker would be of equal importance for anyone endeavoring to Dutch Book a race. The term **Dutch Book** implies playing a race in such a way that no matter what horse wins the bettor would show a profit.

Of course, under the parimutuel system of wagering, it is impossible to operate a true Dutch Book. However, many players use a modified version. They try to eliminate enough of what they consider non-contenders so that they can wager on those remaining in such manner as to show a profit regardless of which of their contenders might win.

Example: If the bettor believed he could safely eliminate one of the 9/5 horses in the above illustration, he could then wager proportionately on the remaining four horses so that no matter which horse won he would be certain of coming out ahead. The 35% of play that he eliminated would be sufficient to compensate for the track's 20% share and still leave him with potential winnings of 15% on his overall investment.

Unfortunately, Dutch Booking, even a modified version under the parimutuel system of wagering, is difficult if not impossible. Many players have tried it but I know of none who've succeeded. One reason for the difficulty is that the individual must wait until almost the last minute before betting in order to be certain of what the final odds will be. By doing this he risks getting shut-out. This applies even if he uses the relatively new automated SAM betting machines.

On the other hand, if he doesn't wait he could encounter such drastic fluctuations in the odds as to have his calculations completely upset. This is due to the fact that the **heavy hitters**, the really big bettors, usually delay their action until almost post time. This frequently has the effect of creating dramatic last-minute odds-changes.

A truly good handicapper however, can make money by judiciously selecting and betting proportionately on two or three horses per race that he regards as being the true contenders. But this requires a high degree of skill and the ability to choose the type race that affords the best opportunity.

My approach, when I regard two horses in a race as being near-equal possibilities, is to first note their odds. Assume one is 3/1 and the other is 7/1. I then ask myself what their odds would be if they ran as a stable entry.

If I conclude, for example, that they probably would be no higher than 1/1, I then would decide that they present a betting opportunity.

My reasoning is that if I bet $20.00 on each under the present conditions, and the shorter-priced 3/1 wins, I get back $80.00.

On the other hand, if the 7/1 horse wins I'd regard it as a bonus. I'd be getting back $160.00, the equivalent of 3/1 odds for my $40.00 investment. If this was a true entry, there would be no chance of getting 3 to 1 odds.

7. BASIC TIPS FOR THE NON-HANDICAPPER

This tome is directed primarily at the initiated fan who, at the least, knows how to read the *Daily Racing Form*. However, even the dyed-in-wool raceplayer may occassionally attend the track with a friend or friends unfamiliar with racing and handicapping. Such guests may not wish to badger their host with innumerable questions, yet they want to have fun too, and maybe win a dollar or two. Okay, this chapter is intended as a guide for such individuals.

There are any number of silly ways that a horse bettor could stumble upon for making selections: He could like a horse's looks: He could be partial to the color red in a jockey's silks: He could like the horse's name or he could play his "lucky" number - on and on.

Going along with any one of these off-beat means of selection could even prove productive during a one-time visit. However, we'd like to offer a few suggestions that will provide the tyro with a sounder base for selecting.

Consulting the "Experts"

The most obvious thing for the uninitiated to do at the track is consult the "experts." That is to say he or she can buy a daily paper such as New York's Daily News or the Los Angeles Times, turn to the sport's section and note who the professional handicappers favor, or buy one of the several tip sheets sold at the tracks.

Will this prove helpful?

Yes! In most cases it will serve to pinpoint the true contenders.

Will it necessarily produce profits? No!

These men know their business and considering the disadvantages they labor under, do a very good job indeed. Their greatest disadvantage is that they are obliged to handicap for every race. No one that the Lord ever created can play every race, every day for an extended period of time and show a flat-bet profit. The term **flat bet** means betting the same amount every time. Flat bets are the universal standard that one's productivity at the track is usually judged by.

Racing's format is such that some races simply are not subject to handicapping.

Example: Many 2-year-old and even 3-year-old maiden races pose nothing more than a question mark inasmuch as many of the entries may be first-time starters; meaning they have never raced, and are of totally unknown quality. Such races present guessing matches, pure and simple.

Many races run on grass (as opposed to dirt) contain horses that have never run on the turf. These too offer an unknown factor that precludes analytical handicapping.

In other contests the majority of horses either haven't run recently or they are competing at the current circuit for the first time, and offer only questionable means for comparison with the local equines.

Fields limited to five or six horses, including favorites at prohibitively short prices, also present extremely risky propositions that quite often prove to be a player's nemesis.

These are just samplings of the type races that the knowledgeable punter avoids. He knows that trying to pick a winner under such adverse conditions has nothing to do with logical handicapping. Luck is the only ingredient involved.

Nonetheless a newspaper handicapper MUST make selections for all races. Furthermore, he does not have the benefit of knowing last minute changes such as late scratches, jockey switches, track condition, and so forth. Suffice then to say, that all things considered, most public selectors do a creditable job, *but invariably will show losses over any extended period of time* .

But, they do know their business. Some, in fact, are very good and the novice could do worse than be guided by their selections. However, try confining your play on their choices to those races which appear to be other than those described in the foregoing.

Handicapping with Raw Earnings

Many track programs offer a considerable amount of helpful information. This information includes showing how many starts each horse has had for the current year and how much in earnings each has managed to accumulate. For example, it might indicate that Horse A ran 12 times and grossed $12,000.00.

Now, somewhat similar to what transpires with humans, a thoroughbred's earnings frequently reflect its ability or class. That is to say that the classier equine worker will average greater earnings for its efforts than the less classy. This, in the same way that the day laborer tends to earn less per hours of effort than the doctor or lawyer.

This being so, and class being a major ingredient of handicapping, one could do far worse than to use earnings as a guide to help them in their efforts to select a winner.

An over-simplified approach is to use the raw earnings figures as provided by the track program. Merely divide the gross earnings (indicated on the program) by the number of times the animal has run.

Example: Horse B ran 12 times and shows earnings of $48,000. If we divide this $48,000 by 12 we arrive at a figure of $4,000. This $4,000 means that B was capable of averaging $4,000 per race each time it ran. We now check the earnings of Horse C in the same manner and conclude that it has a rating of merely $3,000 meaning it had the capability of averaging only $3,000 per race.

The foregoing arithmetics could be applied to each entry in a race, and the horse that produced the highest average or rating would be the selection. This is based on the assumption that the highest earner is intrinsically the best horse. This is not a bad way to "handicap."

Your scribe once did a check of some 200 races and found that if one bet the top earner in each race, according to this formula, a flat-bet loss of only about 7% accrued. We use the word *only* advisedly because a 7% loss compares favorably with the public's overall loss of about 20%.

In actuality, a horse's average earnings do not always directly reflect an animal's class. Quite often it will have as much to do with the trainer's ability as it has to do with the animal itself. Some trainers know where to run their charges to extract the most financial benefit from each race, while others appear to suffer a lack in this area of good judgement.

Parlay Betting

Possibly the most sensible suggestion that could be offered to the infrequent track attendee would be to play parlays. A **parlay** means the combining of the winnings accrued from one bet with those accrued from another. Example: A $2.00 bet on Horse A returns $4.00. The entire $4.00 is then bet on Horse B. This is the simplest form of a parlay. Other combinations can incorporate three, four or more selections.

Now, a major advantage to a parlay is that it's possible to win a relatively large sum of money with minimum risk. Also, at many tracks, a parlay bet can conveniently be made in the form of a single wager. This as opposed to physically having to go to a betting window after each race in order to reinvest whatever returns might have been achieved.

Aside from the convenience of using the special tickets that enable parlay bets to be made as single transactions, there is also a financial benefit involved in using these tickets.

If one were to make a $2.00 wager on Horse X and it won paying $6.00, we could reasonably assume that considerable breakage was deducted prior to the payout (Remember - breakage is the term used for the odd pennies that the track keeps).

In our example the breakage might well have totaled 18

cents. This is what would happen to the first part of a parlay bet if each wager had to be made separately. The same thing would then occur with each successive winning bet that followed in the parlay.

Assume a 4-horse parlay. This could mean that four times 18 cents had been deducted from the total play.

On the other hand, if one uses the track's Parlay Slip, he or she is not only offered its convenience but avoids having breakage deducted for each step involved in the parlay. This means that in our example, the full $6.18 accrued from the bet on Horse X would go onto the second selection in our parlay, and this would continue every step of the way up until the final payoff.

Then, if we assume that a final total was achieved of $60.22, only a mere two cents would be deducted for all of the bets that were involved.

The track's Parlay Slips offer a slight financial advantage to those fans who incline toward this type of wagering. And, in racing one needs to avail themselves of every possible advantage.

Another attribute of the parlay ticket is that it voids the chance of the bettor having a change of heart or getting cold feet. Sort of like the military, once you commit yourself, you're in for the duration.

But most important, parlay betting offers the prospect of plenty of excitement and, as stated, an opportunity to reap a considerable benefit with only minor risk. The following is our suggestion as to how this might be achieved.

How to Bet a Parlay Slip

The track's Parlay Slips allow the bettor to include up to six horses (six races) in a parlay.

Okay! You don't wish to lose any meaningful sum, and still it would be nice if you could win something worthwhile. Right? Of course.

Here's what you do:

Indicate on your slip that you are betting $1.00 total. You

then pick a horse for each of the first six race. Select them via any device that pleases you. Indicate that you want to bet them for show (to run third).

Next, fill out another slip exactly the same way except you now exclude Race One, and start with Race Two and add Race Seven to your second slip. Do the same thing with a third parlay slip, but this time eliminate Race Two and in its place include Race Eight. Then fill out a fourth slip excluding Race Three and this time including the ninth race which in New York is the finale.

You have now invested the grand total of $4.00 and have four separate 6-horse parlays going. If, by some miracle, all nine of your horses ran third or better you'd amass a small fortune - a very small fortune.

For example, if you were fortunate enough to have your first 6-horse parlay click, and IF they averaged even money (1/1) you'd get back $64.00 for your initial $1.00 wager, AND still have the remaining three 6-horse parlays going for you with several of the horses already home free. This, of course, is the ideal situation and illustrates the potential involved.

Even if your first horse ran out, you'd still be *alive* (as us horseplayers so succinctly put it) with your three remaining "strings."

However, the suggestion here is that you don't stop with a $4.00 investment. Let's really splurge and go for broke. Let's buy three more $1.00 parlay tickets as follows anticipating that our first four choices might prove to be *stiffs* as track jargon might express it.

> **Parlay Ticket No. 5** - 5, 6, 7, 8, 9
> **Parlay Ticket No. 6** - 6, 7, 8,
> **Parlay Ticket No. 7** - 7, 8, 9

Assuming one's average selection pays even money, it might be advisable to stop with "Ticket 7" due to the fact that this last parlay would be the only remaining one that could still produce an overall profit even if we lost out on out first six parlay tickets.

We, at this point, would have invested $7.00 and still have the possibility of getting back $8.00 if our 7th ticket clicked.

Of course a $1.00 profit is nothing to grow ecstatic about but it sure beats losing.

Now, if our make-believe bettor lost the 7th parlay too, and was a glutton for punishment, he or she could make a final three dollar parlay bet combining the 8th and 9th races. If this last bet scored the prospective return would be $18.00.

Thus, our valiant punter, who invested only a total $10, could then still emerge with a profit from this den of iniquity.

On the one hand, the worse case-scenario is that the player had a lot of fun, and an exciting day of anticipation that cost only $10.00, or he or she might have gotten lucky and made a profit without having to go for broke.

Just two points to keep in mind. First: The foregoing suggests show betting as offering the best possibility enabling the parlay strings to succeed. Further, it's suggested that all races with favorites that are likely to be less than 8/5 should be avoided.

For example: If the newspaper consensus of opinion indicates a "Best Bet," the horse involved will probably be a very short price at post time.

The chances are unlikely, in such circumstances, that a show bet would average anywhere near even-money. And, that's our second point. Remember that our entire plan is premised on the assumption that one can average even-money overall.

Achieving this average is somewhat akin to Hercules attempting to clean out the Augean stables. But, he succeeded and so can you.

One final point. It's permissible to mix place and show bets, or even win, place and show bets on your parlay tickets but we don't advise this for the purpose outlined in the foregoing.

8. HOW NOT TO SELL A TIP SHEET

The reference to "tip sheets" in the foregoing chapter reminds me of my one and only experience in this area. The thought occured that it might be of interest to the reader. However, bear in mind that I was very young.

During the late Forties, New York's racing season ran from April 15th through November 1st. This left the winter months for horse players to augment their bankrolls and dream up new ways to go from nags to riches.

One particular winter I devoted considerable time to planning a "tip sheet" which I intended to sell at the track. There were eight races a day, but I chose to select only seven in order that my card could conform to its name; "The Lucky Seven."

Selling information within the vicinity of the track was illegal. Despite this, there invariably would be five or six men at each entrance loudly hawking their wares. Understandably they only engaged in this activity when a racing meet was in progress. I felt that if others could sell selections in this manner there was no reason I couldn't do the same.

I paid an artist to create an attractive layout that allowed space for me to fill in the names of fresh horses each day with the aid of a portable Rollaway Press. The card was priced at 50 cents. I calculated that with the aid of one helper I should be able to net a minimum of $30 daily, for a maximum of three hours work; good pay for the times.

When the big day finally arrived I was enthused, and anxious to get started. The only potential flaw was Vinny, my helper. I had reluctantly "hired" him because everyone else I knew had jobs. However, I assured myself, there wasn't much he could do to louse things up. I was shortly to learn that I underestimated him.

The plan was that Vinny would work one gate while I worked another. He would get 50% of everything he sold. My only concern was if the established gentry would resent our presence and try to strong arm us. I didn't know what the situation was, or what to expect, but figured we'd find out soon enough.

Vinny was a good-looking guy, 25 years old, but with a brain that most charitably could be described as dinosaurian. His great concern was a toothbrush that he carried in his pocket and put to use at least a dozen times daily — whether he ate anything or not. He was proud of his teeth and smiled frequently to make sure no one would be denied the privilege of viewing his 32 little masterpieces. At night his lips were so tired from being extended all day he couldn't move them to read his latest copy of Fantastic Comics.

The evening prior to the great adventure was spent carefully doping out selections and inserting horses' names into "The Lucky Seven" cards. I completed 100, 60 for me and 40 for my assistant.

We arrived at the track at 11:30 A.M., just as the gates opened. The first race was 1:30 P.M. Vinny went to his assigned gate and I to mine. Overcoming my self-consciousness, and apprehension I joined the other barkers in their frenzied bellowing, and was soon bellowing with the best of them. No one tried to interfere. In fact, everyone was quite friendly.

The crowd and my sales went in tandem. Both began with a trickle, but gradually started to flow. I happily anticipated a flood by post time. During the first slow hour I sold 20 cards and was confident the remaining 40 would sell during the last 60 minutes when the crowd coming in would be heaviest.

Just as I'm wondering how Vinny was doing I feel a tap on my shoulder, and there he was. "Bob," he says, "let's get a cupa java." I'm a pretty patient guy, but this jerk could easily have taxed my patience. "For Chrisake, Vinny, you've got all afternoon to drown yourself in coffee. Why go now when we're just getting busy?"

I dreaded the big question but forced myself. "How many cards did you sell?" "I didn't sell nuttin'," he tells me. "Well geez, why don't you get back there and make a buck while you still can?"

"Okay," he replies, and shuffles off with all the haste of a geisha girl out for a leisurely stroll.

Not more than 10 minutes after this dreary conversation I sensed something was wrong. My fellow purveyors of truth had ceased ballyhooing their wares and seemed to be evaporating.

The fellow who had worked nearest me came over and said, "You better put your cards away. Hide them in your pocket." When asked why he explained that the cops were making pick-ups. Periodically they'd stage a "raid" and by tacit agreement try to nab one representative from each card.

"Did they get anyone this time?", I asked. "Just one," he tells me. "Some guy at a gate on the other side." There were probably eight entrances to the old Jamaica Racetrack. Opening day there were at least five vendors at each of them selling tip sheets and cards. This - in case you weren't counting - adds up to a minimum of forty. How then did I know **positively** - with odds of 39 to 1 against me - that Vinny was the one picked up? I'm not clairvoyant, but there was no question in my mind.

My sales amounted to only $12.00 and the day was obviously shot because the cops continued to circulate. I asked one of them which precinct they ordinarily took us criminals to. His non-answer was, "It all depends." I was obliged to spend 60 cents on nickel phone calls before finally learning that Vinny had been vanned to a precinct near the back end of Brooklyn.

By the time I finished with the telephone, ate lunch, went back to the office for more money, and managed to find my way to where he was incarcerated, it was close to 6:00 P.M. I paid a fine of $15 which meant the day was not only a total waste, but had actually cost me $3 plus sundry other expenses.

To top it off, I had to listen to Jerky all the way back to Jamaica complaining because I took so long to get him out.

Not one word of thanks, or apology.

I don't forsake a good idea too readily, but in this case I cravenly threw in the towel and yelled, "Quits!" I was sure there must be easier ways to make a buck, and chalked up the episode to experience. "Sometimes in life," I told myself, "you gotta be philosophic."

Thus ended my only venture in selling selections at a race-track.

9. HOW TO EVALUATE A TRAINER

Unquestionably, the trainer is the most important individual in racing. It is on his or her shoulders that the success or failure of a racing venture rests.

One might compare the trainer to the director of a Broadway production. The **star** is the jockey. He's the one in the limelight. The owner is the **backer** or "angel," the one who pays the bills.

However, it is the trainer who bears total responsibility for the success or failure of a stable. He supervises the training of the horse. He engages jockeys. He hires the stable help, and he is the one obliged to deal with frequently difficult owners. Additionally, he is either an experienced amateur vet or is the one accountable for retaining the services of a professional to tend the many ills that can befall a thoroughbred.

There are as many variations of trainers as there are colors of the rainbow. Some are competent. Some are merely adequate, and still others are totally incompetent. It behooves the player to ascertain for himself the capabilities of the various conditioners who habitually favor his local merry-go-round

Aside from the question of competency, there is also the factor of specialization. Even a superficial study of trainers will show that — within their own range of ability — many seem to perform best in some particular phase of racing.

That is to say, one might excel with turf runners. Another might seem to win most often when dealing with routers on dirt, while still a third would appear to specialize in the handling of sprinters, or 2-year-olds. A prime example serving to support this concept is offered via one of New York's outstanding train-ers; John Veitch who can boast of a 7-year win average of 20%.

Prior to embarking on the writing of this tome, an analysis of Veitch's then current performance revealed an interesting pat-tern. Sufficient races were involved to imply that the results were more than coincidence. During the period surveyed, John Veitch raced horses in New York a total of 247 times. 63 of these races were sprints, and l84 were routes. An overall total of 40 wins were achieved equalling an extremely good average of 16%.

Of Veitch's 247 races, 63 involved sprint distances. He won exactly three of these for a surprisingly low 4.8%. Opposed to this mediocre showing, his l84 route races produced 37 wins for a most respectable 20.1% average. This may have been an out-of-the-ordinary circumstance but would nonetheless serve to caution a player against betting Veitch's horses in sprints, and to give them added attention when they go a route.

Another example is offered to underscore the necessity to study a trainer's strengths and weaknesses. Overall, Oscar Barrera can boast of a most laudable winning percentage that hovers around the 16% mark. This means he scores with about one out of every six horses that he enters, and considering the vast number that he runs, this is indeed outstanding.

However, a check of training records published by Blood-stock Research of Lexington, Kentucky, reveals that during the period surveyed, Barrera had 173 starts on turf, but showed only six wins. This is an average of 3% compared to one out of six wins overall. Obviously one would be well-advised to be cautious when betting Barrera's horses in turf races.

The foregoing examples are cited to show that it is as impor-tant to study the past performances of trainers as it is to study those of the thoroughbreds in their charge.

The Owner's Viewpoint

A good way to improve one's perspective of trainers is to place one's self in the position of an owner. The logical way to proceed when hiring a trainer would be the same as any businessman normally would when seeking to fill an executive position. He would require a resume that would outline the applicant's capabilities.

But, through some quirk of human nature, this logical process does not seem to apply in racing. Owners frequently engage trainers on the basis of personality, heresay, whim, or simply via persuasion by the trainer himself. With so much information readily available today — via computerized hi-tech services and data banks — it's surprising that this situation prevails. Practically any information one seeks, relative to thoroughbred racing, is conveniently at hand. This availability certainly applies to trainer's performance records.

Years ago the serious racing fan, who realized the importance of such information, was compelled to maintain his own records. This involved considerable time and attention. Nowadays such effort is no longer necessary. Various data banks have the capability of supplying an astounding amount of information — for a price, of course.

The questionable hiring practices of many owners are not the only source of wonderment in racing. When one considers the high cost of maintaining a thoroughbred at a major circuit; when one considers the fact that there is not — by any means — sufficient purse monies available to cover overhead for the majority of stables (even many of the more "successful" ones), it becomes a question as to why so many who foot the bills still remain in the game. It's a matter of record that the vast majority of owners lose money year in and year out.

Why then do they remain? To some, racing represents a tax write-off. To others it's a matter of prestige. To many of the wealthy it's simply family tradition. Some regard racing as a social event to which they bring their family and friends; while to still others racing is in their blood, and there's always tomorrow which offers hope that things will change. After all, that newly acquired 2-year-old could be the next Kentucky Derby winner.

Regardless, what we're suggesting is that the player who contemplates a bet should try putting himself mentally in the place of the owner of the horse involved, and ask himself two basic questions before each race:

1. Has this trainer evinced sufficient capability to warrant my confidence if I actually was the owner?

2. Would this be the spot where I'd approve of running the horse if a win was sought (as opposed to it being a mere conditioning or "tightening" race)?

If the answers to both questions are negative, the bettor would be well advised to pass the race.

THE TWO CATEGORIES OF TRAINERS

Claiming Trainers

Another important consideration relative to thoroughbred conditioners is that of their primary background. Some trainers such as Pete Ferriola, "Butch" Lenzini and Oscar Barrera are essentially **haltermen** or **claiming trainers**. They specialize in claiming horses (usually from lesser horsemen) and then endeavoring to improve them to an extent where the claim becomes profitable. Each circuit has its own group of such specialists.

An outstanding example of a profitable claim is that of King's Swan who was haltered by Dick Dutrow in New York for $80,000, and, at this writing, appears well on his way to chalking up a gross of $2,000,000 in earnings before being retired. An older example from the Fifties is that of Stymie who was claimed for $1,500 by Hall-Of-Famer Hirsch Jacobs, and who went on to amass almost a million dollars in purses at a time when such a sum represented real money.

Elite Trainers

Another group of trainers could be classified as "the elite." Representative of this group are Wayne Lucas, "Woody" Stephens, Claude McGaughey, and Charlie Whittingham. Such trainers invariably work for wealthy individuals and have near-unlimited funds backing them. They are as far removed from claiming trainers as night is from day. This, however, does not imply that one group's talents are superior to the other. Each has its own set of required skills.

Somewhat surprisingly, when trainers from either category, for one reason or another, leave their particular realm of expertise, they seldom do well. Circumstances undoubtedly play a part, but the fact remains that a claiming trainer put in charge of a "fashionable" stable rarely proves to be a shining light.

Frank Martin, a noted halterman, held New York's leading trainer title for 10 years, and yet when he severed connections with Mrs. Sommer, his long-time sponsor, and went to work for non-claiming Harbor View Farm, he didn't exactly set the world on fire.

Even Hall-of-Fame trainer Allen Jerkens, who was obliged to assemble a "public stable" after working for many years almost exclusively for Jack Dreyfus's Hobeau Farm, had problems getting oriented to claimers.

The fact is that in racing, claiming horses and non-claiming horses - along with the men and women who guide their destiny - would seem to function in almost totally different atmospheres.

Those trainers fortunate enough to handle thoroughbreds for wealthy clients enjoy many advantages over most claiming trainers.

Foremost is the fact that they can afford the best of everything, and in racing, this equates with greater opportunities for winning. Wealthy stables can afford the best stable help, the best feed that money can buy, the best blacksmiths, the best vets and the best exercise riders. Each factor is an important one in preparing an animal for a winning effort.

Possibly THE most important edge that such trainers enjoy is the fact that they can afford to rotate their stock. Unlike many claiming outfits, they don't have to risk running their charges ragged in order to pay feed bills.

Additionally, successful trainers, particularly those employed by wealthy patrons, have the privilege of being able to choose their spots. Unlike many of the less-successful, they aren't forced to run horses where they know they don't belong. Many times a hard-up trainer will enter his charge with little more than a hope and a prayer that it might, through some fluke, garner at least a portion of the purse.

Also, in many instances the "little guy" is pressured by the track secretary to enter a horse just to round out a field or insure that there will be enough horses to allow for an exacta pool. The pressure exerted, which is usually tacit is, "Cooperate if you want to maintain stall space." Such pressure cannot be exerted against a successful barn that has options not available to the less successful.

A third major benefit enjoyed by those conditioners who work for affluent stables is that usually they can afford to be independent and demand to be allowed to train without interference from an owner. Too often, less successful trainers are obliged, against their better judgement, to give in to owners who think they know more than their trainers.

Judging A Trainer's Capabilities

If one does not choose - or does not own the necessary computer, modem, and software - to avail him or herself of a racing data-bank service, he can still compile his own records to keep track of the trainers who race at a favored circuit. This involves time and some effort. However, it is time well spent if what one learns is heeded and practiced.

Fortunately, most track programs now provide information in the form of periodic summaries relative to both trainer and jockey performances. At the end of any single fiscal (betting?) year one should have been able to accumulate enough statistics from this source alone to provide a good idea of how the various trainers stack up.

One might choose to categorize trainers as falling within one of four classifications:

HOW TO EVALUATE A TRAINER

> **Trainer Rating Chart**
> 1. 20% or greater wins is deemed superior
> 2. 15% to 20% is above average
> 3. 10% to 15% wins is about normal
> 4. Below 10% should be considered with care

But, these figures apply over the long term. Don't judge a trainer on the basis of one short meeting. Like you and I, trainers too are subject to periodic slumps. In racing as in many other areas one should be prepared to cope with unavoidable streaks.

There is however, a caveat to this percentage business. Keep in mind that volume too must be a consideration. If a trainer enters only 10 horses over a period of a year and wins four times for a 40% average, his accomplishment should be judged with caution.

On the other hand, a trainer who races 300 or more times (many do), and manages to chalk up 15% wins is doing exceptionally well.

10. HOW TO EVALUATE A JOCKEY

The little men who do the booting are 4-star athletes. Make no mistake about it. Up to nine times a day they are required to use their average weight of about 110 pounds to control 1,000 or more pounds of solid muscle that's running at a rate approximating 40 miles an hour. This is no job for the physically unfit, or the timid.

Jockeys are obliged to work under frequently hazardous conditions, and literally face the possibility of serious injury or death every time they mount a horse. Slippery track conditions, a horse that suddenly breaks down, unintended jostling in a crowded race field; any one of these situations pose a threat to a riders' life and limb.

On the other hand, the best of them who ride at the major ovals are generously compensated and have per annum earnings that almost - but not quite - approximate those of the top stars in boxing, baseball and football.

It is this scribes belief that jockeys deserve what they earn, not only due to the risks involved but due to the purse monies they win for the people who use their services. Let me emphasize though that this applies to the upper echelon of jockeydom.

As in every field, the business of chauffeuring thoroughbreds has its quota of varying stratas of ability. There is the best, the merely capable, the mediocre, and the near-useless.

Current day riding luminaries such as Angel Cordero, erstwhile American jockey Steve Cauthen, and just-retired Bill Shoemaker had their counterparts in times past. In previous decades it was people such as Eddie Arcaro, John Longden, Ted

Atkinson, Earl Sande and Don Meade. The only real difference in the racing scene is that the current-day riders include top female performers. Outstanding in this category is Julie Krone who time and again has demonstrated her ability to boot 'em home with the very best.

What are these special abilities that all top riders seem to possess?

Attributes of a Top Jockey

1. It must be presumed that, like a good thoroughbred trainer, they have the knack of establishing rapport with the normally high-strung, temperamental animals with which they deal.

2. Their reflexes must be above par, giving them the ability to make instantaneous correct decisions as either opportunity or necessity dictates during the running of a race.

3. They must possess what in slang terms is called "guts." When a split-second opening occurs in a race, in what previously loomed as a solid wall of horseflesh, they must have the nerve to try to get through rather than lose precious real estate by pulling their mount up, and going around.

Also, it's vital that their co-workers know that they can't be intimidated during the running of a race, and that if the occasion demands they are the ones who will do the intimidating.

4. They must have the ability to judge pace. A fast pace can dictate one strategy, a slow early pace can call for another. Even the better exercise boys, or jockeys if they work a horse or horses in the morning, must be able to heed a trainer's instructions.

If he calls for a workout of 4-furlongs in 48 seconds (even time), he'd be furious if the horse was clocked in 45 and 3/5th seconds. He might fear that the animal, by being worked too fast in the A.M., could risk losing its racing edge.

There's still a fifth factor.

5. Many knowledgeable horsemen concur that a horse is capable of just one big run per race. The cheaper animal might have the ability to make this one major effort for a sixteenth of a mile, whereas the superior thoroughbred's top speed might hold for a full eighth or even a quarter of a mile.

Personally, I subscribe to this theory, and from having observed many thousands of races over the years, I've concluded that possibly THE major asset a jockey can have is knowing at what strategic stage of the race he should allow his mount to unleash its big run.

Many times I've had the feeling, even when watching races that I had no financial interest in, that Horse X or Horse Y was given its head prematurely and had nothing left for the final drive.

The better jocks do not make this mistake as often as the lesser lights. This applies particularly when they know their mount. For this reason, aside from others, I'm partial to a horse ridden by a booter who has ridden it before and knows the animal's quirks.

It's this writer's opinion that a jockey's relative ability becomes manifest in direct ratio to the distance of a race. That is to say that one's ability, or the lack of it, assumes greater importance as distance is increased.

Most apprentices have the capability to break a horse fast which is the prime requisite in sprint races. In consequence the majority of their wins are usually acquired under such circumstances. In route races they usually do not fare as well, not necessarily because they are lacking in basic ability but because they are lacking in the experience necessary for properly gauging pace.

An experienced and skilled booter not only will be able to correctly gauge the pace of a race, but quite often, by controlling the pace, he can enable a front-running sprinter to go a route. This strategy would be accomplished via the tactical maneuver of deliberately holding the front-runner back, and setting early fractions deceptively slow. The end result would then be that a route race was effectively turned into a sprint affair inasmuch as the real racing wasn't done until after the final half-mile or so.

An oft quoted maxim is, "It's the pace that kills." This implies that even a confirmed sprinter could run all day if the pace was slow enough.

6. There's still another major asset possessed by the competent, experienced journeyman that a **bug boy** (apprentice) lacks. He quite often can provide a number of helpful suggestions to the trainer based on what he observed during the running of a race.

Example: He may point out that he had a problem getting the animal to change leads, meaning that the horse continued leading with its left leg as opposed to correctly switching to the right going around a turn. Or - maybe he sensed that the thoroughbred reacted negatively to the use of the whip, and would do better next time if given just a hand ride.

Checking the Record

We've reproduced statistics on the following page that show the final jockey standings for a recent Aqueduct Winter Meet. Many track programs provide similar, up-to-date stats for the benefit of their patrons.

It's strongly suggested that such figures be studied carefully. A lot can be learned by the fan who's willing to break down the raw figures and convert them into something more meaningful. They cannot be accepted at face value.

Example: This was the first New York venture for Mike Smith who migrated here from the Chicago area. Taking this fact into consideration it was remarkable that he did so well. And, his performance was even better during the Spring Meet that followed.

Most newcomers, regardless of ability, need considerable time to establish contacts, and get a foothold.

However, when examining a performance report, whether it relates to trainers or to jockeys, more emphasis should be placed on the percentage of wins rather than the sheer number.

Also, and this applies to trainers too, volume should be a major consideration. A jockey or trainer might get lucky and sustain a high winning average for 10 or 20 races, but the luck element tends to dissipate as the numbers increase. If a jockey

HOW TO WIN AT HORSERACING

Jockey And Trainer Standings
Final Aqueduct Winter Meet

Jockey	Mts.	1st	2nd	3rd	W%	Fv%	Spr	Dist	Lsts
Cordero, Jr.	224	52	41	30	.23	.38	29-130	23-94	8-22
Smith	355	46	52	58	.13	.28	20-190	26-165	3-26
Santos	234	41	39	36	.18	.31	27-131	14-103	1-27
Bruin	274	41	33	35	.15	.35	19-147	22-127	5-28
Chavez	271	37	51	26	.14	.27	15-148	22-123	2-34
Velasquez	273	36	21	34	.13	.30	13-138	23-135	4-22
Morales	205	35	20	29	.17	.38	20-110	15-95	2-15
Samyn	193	28	27	21	.15	.35	12-92	16-101	0-17
Madrid, Jr.	214	25	24	20	.12	.38	11-114	14-100	6-19
Rojas	169	23	17	20	.14	.32	9-68	14-101	3-17
Aquila *	191	19	22	25	.10	.11	10-98	9-93	3-15
Toscano *	195	19	20	35	.10	.23	10-112	9-83	1-20
Santagata	205	18	20	21	.09	.36	10-117	8-88	1-16
Maple	143	17	16	20	.12	.33	7-75	10-68	2-11
Ferrer	109	13	12	16	.12	.44	7-56	6-53	2-15
Medero *	124	12	16	7	.10	.50	8-68	4-56	1-10
Thibeau, Jr.	88	11	8	6	.13	.20	8-48	3-40	0-6
Fell	99	9	5	6	.09	.33	4-52	5-47	1-11
Lovato, Jr.	124	8	14	4	.06	.33	6-57	2-67	0-10
Collazo *	71	6	9	5	.08	.50	6-40	0-31	1-7
Lydon *	76	6	2	3	.08	.25	4-41	2-35	1-9
Carr	107	6	8	9	.06	.00	4-64	2-43	0-14
Razo, Jr.	73	5	4	9	.07	.50	4-38	1-35	2-12
LaBoccetta, Jr.*	73	5	4	7	.07	1.00	2-40	3-33	1-11

*Apprentice Jockey

Trainer	Sts.	1st	2nd	3rd	W%	Fv%	Spr	Dist	Lsts
Moschera	94	21	16	11	.22	.38	13-55	8-39	0-11
Klesaris	72	20	15	12	.28	.29	13-45	7-27	4-10
Barrera	135	17	17	11	.13	.21	8-70	9-65	3-18
Odintz	53	15	5	10	.28	.50	13-33	2-20	2-8
DiMauro	102	12	7	8	.12	.38	6-51	6-51	0-9
Lukas	68	11	14	10	.16	.32	5-37	6-31	0-8
Lake	76	11	11	11	.14	.11	10-53	1-23	1-11
Dutrow	90	11	8	12	.12	.27	7-57	4-33	3-9
F. Martin	55	10	7	5	.18	.50	1-25	9-30	3-7
Ferriola	39	9	8	6	.23	.83	8-23	1-16	3-9
J. Martin	42	9	6	7	.21	.44	2-14	7-28	1-6
Barbara	60	9	11	11	.15	.27	8-47	1-13	0-7
Johnson	60	9	8	8	.15	.25	3-21	6-39	1-7

scores with four wins out of 10 races this is not necessarily meaningful. When he wins 100 races out of 500 it can reasonably be assumed that he merits a top rating.

On this basis then, Smith did not do quite as well as the raw figures might suggest. His achievement was due as much to hard work as it was to raw ability. This, by no means, diminishes his accomplishment but nonetheless should be examined in the proper context. For example: Mike Smith rode 355 horses and scored with 46 which put him only six below Angel Cordero's 52 wins.

But, the fact is that the durable Angel had only 224 mounts and won with a high 23% average while Mike Smith's 355 mounts enabled him to average only 13%. Summed up, we're stating that both trainer and jockey performances should be measured more in terms of volume and percentages as opposed to that which is evinced by just the raw win numbers.

On this basis let's revise the foregoing list and see how the top 10 shape up.

Top 10 Jockeys - Aqueduct 89-90	
Cordero	23%
Santos	18%
Morales	17%
Bruin	15%
Samyn	15%
Chavez	14%
Rojas	14%
Smith	13%
Velasquez	13%
Madrid	13%

Also, aside from suggesting a close examination of the raw win figures, I further suggest that the place hole figures also be studied. Wrongfully or otherwise, I have a strong preference for those riders who do well in the second slot. In part, this is because I do quite a bit of place betting.

Good percentage figures in this area assure me that when I make a place bet I'll get a run for my money.

A reasonable criterion for gauging this aspect of a jock's

performance is to compare his win and place averages. If we again glance at the original stats we can see that Smith, Chavez, Samyn and Madrid, among the top 10, hold up very well when this is our standard.

A Minor Group Ride a Majority of Winners

There's still another criterion that this table offers for evaluating performance. Glance at the figures for sprints and routes. Note the performance variances that frequently show up between the two.

As an example, and in line with one of our previous comments relative to apprentices versus journeymen - glance at the performance figures for Lois Collazo. His overall win percentage is a highly creditable 8% keeping in mind that he's still serving an apprenticeship. Six out of 40 wins were achieved in sprints equal to a very good 15% average.

On the other hand, checking his route performance we find he failed to win even once in 31 tries. This probably is not so much a reflection on the young man's ability as it is on the fact that his agent couldn't convince trainers to put him on "live" ones in distance affairs. Nonetheless, this serves to dramatize the fact that such discrepancies do exist and the player is well advised to learn to whom they apply.

We still have a final point to bring out. New York usually has about 60 regular riders on hand including apprentices. If you glance again at the table for the Winter Meet jockey standings you'll see that the tabulations involved a total of 518 races. Of these, 364 were won by the top 10 jockeys. This is equal to 70%.

This means that the top 10 riders equalling only 17% of the jockey colony won seven out of every 10 races. Stated another way; 83% of the riders were left with only 30% winners to be shared.

This is by no means unusual. It is what generally prevails and should serve to caution the player to pay close attention to the trainer's choice of rider. Also, in respect to this, many trainers seem to favor certain riders whenever they mean business.

HOW TO EVALUATE A JOCKEY

In New York, as on other circuits, there's a number of train-ers that almost always seem to incline toward a favored jock.

When one notes that this favored rider does not have a leg up, the fan should try to analyze why? Is the stables' "regular" jockey out-of-town? Is it because he's being replaced with an apprentice? Does he have another mount in the same race and had made a previous commitment or did the trainer agree to let him ride a probable winner as opposed, possibly, to the trainer's own entry of dubious quality?

11. THE STRUCTURE OF THOROUGHBRED RACING

Many times over the years I've heard the comment, "They've all got four legs, haven't they?" This bit of cynicism is invariably spouted by the uninitiated and is intended to convey the fact that, like Gertrude Stein's, "A rose, is a rose, is a rose," a race is a race, is a race, therefore any horse can win.

The broader implication is that any horse could win any race because basically they're all structured in similar fashion. Actually this is as silly as saying anyone could win a heavyweight championship fight because everybody has two fists.

The truth is that thoroughbred racing is composed of as many stratas as a tall building, with each strata's class clearly defined. This matter of distinct divisions is what, for example, prevents an overwhelming number of thoroughbreds from being nominated to run in every big money, or glamorous race. If this situation did not exist a prestigious, event such as the Kentucky Derby would have hundreds or even thousands of horses seeking to compete.

Factually, horse racing, as a competitive sport, is so intricately and cleverly constructed that if one took time out to really consider the matter he would have to be impressed.

The actuality, of course, is that no single person or group planned racing. The current successful format was attained over many years, via much trial and error. If one truly wished to trace its history he'd have to go back hundreds of years. However, racing as we know it today got its impetus in the middle of the nineteenth century when an Englishman named Admiral

John Francis Rous devised a scale of weights which tended, quite effectively, to neutralize whatever physical advantages older horses might have over younger ones, or that males might have over females. It also took into consideration such vital factors as distance, and the time of year.

See **Jockey Club Scale of Weights**.

The basics of this scale are employed today in a somewhat modified form by track handicapper-secretaries whose job it is to write the various conditions stipulated for each race. We'll discuss these conditions in the following.

Racing Conditions

The structure of racing is controlled by the various conditions imposed on each race by a race-wise individual employed by a racing association. He is usually referred to as the **Racing Secretary and Handicapper**.

His job, in essence, is to stipulate which horses are eligible to compete in a specific race. These stipulations are known as racing conditions and are carefully outlined in booklets available to horsemen and logically, titled **Condition Books**.

The man employed by a racing association to write the various conditions for a race meeting must not only know racing, but must also know the quality of the horses stabled on the grounds of his particular circuit, and the type horse he might wish to attract or lure away from other circuits.

The Secretary's prime job is to specify conditions that will make racing as competitive as possible, yet still take into consideration the quality of the thoroughbreds available for him to work with. Example: If his circuit doesn't stable $50,000 claiming horses it obviously would be futile to write race conditions designed to attract this quality of thoroughbred.

A condition book is frequently referred to as "The Horseman's Bible." This somewhat facetious reference comes about presumably because a trainer can no more afford to be casual about the condition book than a priest can afford to be casual about the holy book. In both cases they are matters of serious concern. A trainer must study the condition book assiduously if

Jockey Club Scale Of Weights

The following weights are carried when the weights are not stated in the conditions of the race.

Distance	Age	Jan	Feb	Mar	April	May	June	July	Aug	Sept	Oct	Nov	Dec
Half Mile	Two Years	x	x	x	x	x	x	x	105	108	111	114	114
	Three years	117	117	119	119	121	123	125	126	127	128	129	129
	Four years	130	130	130	130	130	130	130	130	130	130	130	130
	Five years & Up	130	130	130	130	130	130	130	130	130	130	130	130
Six Furlongs	Two years	x	x	x	x	x	x	x	102	105	108	111	111
	Three years	114	114	117	117	119	121	123	125	126	127	128	128
	Four years	129	129	130	130	130	130	130	130	130	130	130	130
	Five years & Up	130	130	130	130	130	130	130	130	130	130	130	130
One Mile	Two years	x	x	x	x	x	x	x	x	96	99	102	102
	Three years	107	107	111	111	113	115	117	119	121	122	123	123
	Four years	127	127	128	128	127	126	126	126	126	126	126	126
	Five years & Up	128	128	128	128	127	126	126	126	126	126	126	126
One and a Quarter Miles	Two years	x	x	x	x	x	x	x	x	x	x	x	x
	Three years	101	101	107	107	111	113	116	118	120	121	122	122
	Four years	125	125	127	127	127	126	126	126	126	126	126	126
	Five years & Up	127	127	127	127	127	126	126	126	126	126	126	126
One and a Half Miles	Two years	x	x	x	x	x	x	x	x	x	x	x	x
	Three years	98	98	104	104	108	111	114	117	119	121	122	122
	Four years	124	124	126	126	126	126	126	126	126	126	126	126
	Five years & Up	126	126	126	126	126	126	126	126	126	126	126	126
Two Miles	Three years	96	96	102	102	106	109	112	114	117	119	120	120
	Four Years	124	124	126	126	126	126	126	125	125	124	124	124
	Five Years & Up	126	126	126	126	126	126	126	125	125	124	124	124

he wishes to spot his horses advantageously.

The ability to do this implies that a trainer not only must interpret the conditions properly, but must also be sufficiently aware to be able to surmise which other horses stabled on the grounds will probably be attracted by the same conditions. This, in effect, enables him to size up the competition BEFORE a race. The proper placing of horses is one of the skills that serve to separate the competent from the incompetent trainer.

An example from one of New York's condition books is shown here, but similar information is available from the track programs and in the *Daily Racing Form*. It is provided for each race, each day.

7th Race - Claiming	One Mile
Purse $22,000. For Three-Year-Olds and Upward.	
Three-Year-Olds.....120 lbs.	Older.....122lbs.
Non-Winners of two races at a mile or over	
since October 15 allowed	.....3lbs.
Of such a race since then	.....5 lbs.
Claiming Price $35,000; for each $2,500 to $30,000	.....2 lbs.
(Races when entered to be claimed for $25,000 or less not considered)	

Trainers, as stated (and jockey agents also) are obliged to study race conditions with extreme care if they wish to place their horses (or riders) to best advantage. This being so, it should follow that the serious race player should do no less. Unfortunately this frequently is not the case. Many players who consider themselves handicappers ignore the conditions or at best give them no more than superficial attention. This is a mistake.

Example: Read the conditions given in the foregoing illustration for the 7th race on to be run at one mile. These are fairly standard conditions for a top and bottom claiming race and many players might simply take them for granted. A case of, "If you've seen one you've seen them all." This attitude can prove costly.

Just a few weeks prior to this writing NYRA's racing secretary introduced a kicker into his conditions that went unnoticed by the majority of fans. The usual conditions for a claiming race in New York is shown below and is derived from the track's racing program. It reads in part as follows:

"For four-year-olds and upward. 122 lbs. Non-winners of two races at a mile or over since April 1 allowed 3 lbs.; of such a race since then, 5 lbs."

Note that the stipulations do not prohibit multi-winners from being entered. Now read the conditions imposed by the innovation.

"For four-year-olds and upward WHICH HAVE NEVER WON TWO RACES (then it continues) Non-winners of a race at a mile or over since April 15 allowed 3 lbs, etc."

Now, the claiming values of horses entered in both races might read "Claiming price $25,000; for each $2,500 to $20,000; 2 lbs. (Races when entered to be claimed for $18,000 or less not considered in estimating allowances)."

The point is that to the casual condition reader, or to the non-reader, the quality of horses involved in these two races would be assumed to be similar inasmuch as the claiming prices, distances, age and sex might all be the same. But, there could be a vast difference involved.

One race will attract multi-winners, and the other can only attract horses that, as a group, are inferior. This is so because despite almost three years of racing opportunities they have been able to win only one lone race. And - the chances are that even this one victory was accomplished against maidens of equally poor quality.

This provides merely one example of why a race's conditions should be studied as an automatic reflex when handicapping. Each circuit will have its own unique conditions and no matter how familiar one might feel he is with these, a new element can always be injected.

Racing's Hierarchy

The schema of thoroughbred racing is such as to accomplish two basic purposes.

1. The first is to avoid any horse or small group of horses monopolizing purses.

2. It clearly categorizes horses in such manner as to have like compete against like. This is accomplished via the estab- lishment of clear-cut divisions precluding the likelihood that an inferior animal will be required to run against a champion.

Actually, as we shall see, these two factions go hand in hand.

Maiden Claiming Races

Let's start with the lowest grades and work our way up.

At the bottom rung of the ladder are **Maiden Claiming Races.** These are for 2-year-olds and up who have never won a race, and are eligible to be claimed out of any race of this type in which they are entered.

The claiming of a horse is simply the process of someone putting in a bid to buy a horse prior to a race being run. Once the horses leave the starting gate the party making the suc- cessful bid (the one that's drawn if more than one bid for the same horse has been dropped into the claim box) owns the animal even if it should be injured or drop dead during or immediately after the race has been run.

The conditions involved in claiming races for both winners and maiden claimers are similar in respect to the amounts for which they can be claimed. Usually such races are **top and bottom claimers**.

Example: In a race for horses entered to be claimed for a top price of $35,000 there is usually a two-pound weight off incentive offered for each $2,500 increment down to $30,000. Expressed otherwise, a horse entered for $32,500 would carry two pounds less than a horse entered at the top figure of $35,000. An animal with a $30,000 tag would be given a four- pound advantage based on its lowered claiming price.

The concept underlying the structure of claiming-race condi- tions is a clever one. The very fact that a horse can be bought out of a claiming race, for whatever its claiming price is, dis- courages any trainer attempting to cinch a purse by entering a high-grade animal against those of lesser worth.

A true $75,000 thoroughbred entered in a race for $35,000 horses would be claimed immediately by any one of a number of alert horsemen who are constantly on the prowl for bargains.

On occasion one will note in a claiming race that one of the entries has been dropped considerably in price. It may previously have been running for a $75,000 tag and today is entered for $35,000.

This is a situation that poses a dilemma for the handicapper. Is the **drop-down** unsound and the trainer simply wishes to dispose of it, OR is this a ruse to enable the trainer to steal a purse by fooling other horsemen into believing his horse is unsound?

Actually, what the true situation is, in many cases of drastic drop-downs, is that the trainer is dealing with a thoroughbred that has a chronic disability, but through either his own, or his vet's skill, it still maintains a degree of short term racing condition. It gets moved down the claiming ladder in a genuine attempt to garner a purse, but neither the trainer nor owner would be inconsolable if the animal was haltered.

Claiming trainers generally try to claim from conditioners they regard as being less skilled than themselves. The thinking in most cases is that they know how to cure what is perceived as being wrong with the animal. Many times their information is based on the judgement of a friendly exercise boy, veterinarian, blacksmith or even a jockey.

A sensible trainer operates on the premise that he should never claim a horse from a better trainer, recognizing that it would be unlikely he could improve the performance of such an animal.

Okay, back to our maiden claimers. We've indicated that they represent the lowest strata of the thoroughbred hierarchy. However, even within this group (and in most other categories which we will define) there is a sub-division that should be recognized.

The fact is that even the lowly 2-year-old claimer has a chance to eventually improve. But, when it comes to dealing with more mature maiden-claiming horses such an eventuality becomes unlikely. This is so simply because the older thoroughbred has, in most cases, had many more opportunities to evince ability than the juveniles have had. A 2-year-old maiden-claiming horse may have been to the wars only four times, whereas a 4-year-old may well have been entered unsuccessfully 24 times.

Maiden Special Weights Races

The next rung up the class ladder finds us confronting the **Maiden Special Weights** group. These are thoroughbreds that, like maiden claiming horses, have yet to win a race, but their connections still regard them highly enough that they are unwilling to risk losing them via the claiming route. As with maiden claimers, and most other categories, such races are restricted by age to **2-year-olds** representing one group; **3-year-olds** another group if early in the year, and finally one for **4-year-olds** and up.

Oddly enough, when we use the phrase the "the next rung up the class ladder," it would imply that this group is next to the lowest in class. This is not necessarily the case. All horses start as maidens and it is from these ranks that the champions as well as the mediocrities emerge.

Therefore, depending on several factors, horses competing in Maiden Special Weights races are not necessarily next to the lowest class.

A major factor that influences the quality involved in Maiden Special Weights races is age. Another is the time of year which actually is tied in with the age factor.

Maiden races geared for 2-year-olds are invariably of far higher class than seemingly similar races for older horses. This applies especially during the early part of the year, and is due to reasons previously presented - that - the younger horses have not been given full opportunity to display whatever talents they might possess. On the other hand, particularly as the year progresses, the older horses have, in most cases, had considerable opportunity and have failed to demonstrate ability.

In Special Weight races there are no weight penalties imposed as there are in most other races. The term Special Weights conveys that horses are all assigned scale weight. But, this would not necessarily mean they all actually carry the same weight. There are weight concessions granted for sex (a female entered against males), age (younger horses racing against older horses), and appropriate allowances for the use of an apprentice rider.

Starting around April of each year track secretaries will begin to write race conditions for *3-year-olds and up*, with the younger horses getting weight off according to the previously discussed Scale of Weights.

Females are usually separated by race conditions from having to compete against males. But occasionally, and always voluntarily on the trainer's part, they do compete. Sometimes, but not often, they are successful. Three females have even succeeded in humiliating their male counterparts by winning the Kentucky Derby. An axiom of racing states, "Fillies in the fall." This implies that the fall of the year offers the best prospect for females besting males. I can't vouch that this is so.

Bear in mind that males cannot compete in races for females, but in most cases fillies and mares can volunteer to run against males. Similarly, winners can't run in races conditioned for maidens, but maidens have the option to run against winners.

We've suggested at the beginning of this chapter that the pattern of racing is truly an intricate one, and it should be obvious from just the foregoing discussion of maidens that there is indeed nothing simple about racing's overall format.

Claiming Races

Although we're presenting claiming races as being the next step up on our class ladder this too is subject to qualification inasmuch as claimers quite frequently compete in allowance races, and allowance horses frequently migrate to claimers and back again to allowance affairs.

Broadly speaking, **claiming horses** are those willing to be put at risk to be claimed whereas non-claimers would appear to be valued more highly by their connections.

We've made the point elsewhere that racing tends to rule out the chance that any horse or group of horses will maintain a major advantage over competitors. It was stated that in claiming races this was accomplished primarily due to the likelihood that a trainer who chose to run a horse below its rightful niche would lose the horse via the claiming box.

However, the threat of being haltered is not the only means used in the endeavor to achieve an equitable distribution of purse monies. In thoroughbred racing weight is generally regarded as being a levelling factor.

"Weight will stop a freight train." "Weight brings them all together." Such "truisms" have survived and have been subscribed to by many generations of horsemen.

Allowance, Handicap and Stakes Races

We've discussed maiden claimers, Maiden Special Weights, and straight claiming races. Next in line we come to **Allowance** affairs which we have previously touched on. It was stated earlier that the "master plan" underlying thoroughbred racing was conceived in such manner as to have the sport be as competitive as human ingenuity could make it.

Various devices are used to accomplish this; most prominent being the Scale of Weights and the Condition Book, with the latter proving the most effective. The basis for its various stipulations is to have like compete against like.

Thus, in maiden races non-winners run against other non-winners, and in claimers horses of one grade generally run against those of similar quality.

Probably the most effective conditions devised to keep horses within their own ranks are those written for allowance type races and for Maiden Special Weight races. In claiming races the controls work reasonably well, but a clever trainer, as we've noted, can find ways to gain advantage.

In handicap affairs, where the major reliance is on weight, the controls are not quite as effective inasmuch as they fall short of putting all qualifiers on even a theoretically equal basis.

In stake races, and weight-for-age type events forget about equality. The simple fact is that after a certain point racing's controls are ineffective. That is, they fall short to the extent that they are incapable of bringing a really top quality animal down to the level of its inferior would-be competitors. And, in the same sense, it lacks the ability to raise the inferior horse to a level where it can successfully compete against the good or great horse. It is for this reason that the $500,000-and-up purse monies get distributed among a mere handful of thoroughbreds, leaving the remaining thousands to scrounge for the crumbs that are left.

Allowance Races

But now let's see why allowance races, generally speaking, provide the most effective medium for having like compete against like. In New York, with other circuits having a comparable situation, the desired progress of a thoroughbred might be compared to a human's scholastic ascendency. A person would ideally advance from kindergarten, to grade school, to high school, to college and then on to attaining a doctorate in his specialized field of medicine or engineering. A similarity exists with thoroughbreds.

In the most desirable cases, the thoroughbred gets its start in a Maiden Special Weights race. It wins and gets promoted to an allowance race conditioned for horses who have never won a race other than maiden or claiming.

(In our text we abbreviate the various gradations of allowance races to read **A1, A2, A3 and A-4,** with A1 being the lowest grade and A- 4 the highest.)

Assuming that our equine protagonist wins an A1 race, the next step up is an A2 race for horses that have never won TWO races other than maiden or claimers.

We next come to the A3 type race. Now though, a word of caution, we mentioned earlier in our text that there's considerable overlapping between claiming horses and allowance horses, especially when dealing with 4-year-olds and up early in the year, and then 3-year-olds and up as the year progresses.

This overlapping is of the type that frequently can lead to a relatively cheap claiming horse winning an allowance race, within the A1 category, and less so with the A2 races.

Now though, when it comes to an A3 or A4 type race, the chance of a cheap claimer winning such an affair is unlikely. Yet, among better grade claimers there can be (and often is) considerable back-and-forth traffic involved. In other words, top grade claiming horses frequently compete successfully in top grade allowance races.

At the present time, in New York, a $50,000 claiming price might well provide the line of demarcation serving to differentiate between our labels of "cheap" and "better grade" claimers. Claiming prices on the Big Apple circuit currently offer the following gradations (using the top price in each category): $14,000, $17,500, $25,000, $35,000, $50,000, then $75,000 and finally $100,000.

To this point, assume we've followed our equine hero through successful and successive stages of its career inclusive of winning an allowance race for non-winners of four (which exists but is somewhat rare). At this point the logical alternative would be to run it in "overnight" handicaps. Assuming its success continues, it next might progress to "name" handicaps.

Each successful foray into a higher division means it is competing for bigger and bigger purses. Finally, its connections decide that their charge should no longer be subjected to the increasingly heavy weight packages that the track secretary/handicapper has seen fit to assign.

The only alternative left would be to compete only in stake races that have a ceiling on weights, or in weight-for-age type races wherein all entries carry the same weight.

If we're dealing with a "whole" horse, as opposed to a gelding or ridgling, the final stage in such an animal's ideal career would be to put it to stud whereby it would continue proving its worth as a money machine, probably to even a greater degree than when it raced.

12. CONDITION AS A WINNING EDGE

It can be said without equivocation that current form (condition) should be the foremost consideration of the handicapper. Condition supercedes class, weight, jockeys and just about anything else that could influence a thoroughbred's performance.

But, as always, there's a caveat. How is condition determined?

Of course, if a thoroughbred won its last race recently by 10 lengths, one can reasonably assume the animal is in good form. The catch is that just about everyone else, in both the grandstand and clubhouse, is aware of this fact, and too often such awareness translates into unacceptably low odds.

This is a very important point. One cannot profit from horseracing by going along with the obvious. It's the slightly unorthodox approach that affords the player his best chance to succeed.

For example, a player who notes that a certain horse had a recent speedy (**bullet**) workout has not unearthed a gold nugget. The chances are that everyone else has noted this as well.

Therefore, the odds quoted will take this obvious handicapping information into consideration - the same as would be the case with the 10-length win mentioned above - and void any chance of providing a benefit.

On the other hand, the player who might note that a trainer has switched from an apprentice to a jockey who in the past has ridden the horse successfully will gain a slight edge. This is so because, even though this probably provides a clue to the trainer's intentions, it is not the sort of thing that the public ordinarily heeds.

We cite this as only a minor example intended to emphasize that one should look for valid but less obvious handicapping clues than those that everyone else emphasizes. Keep the thought in mind that if you follow the same path that the betting public follows, you, like the public, must also lose.

But, back now to our physical condition factor. A trainer, quite often, will fail to let a horse reap the full benefit from its good condition. Assume he has a horse that beat a band of $35,000 maidens by the aforementioned 10 lengths. The trainer might be convinced by this display that he has the second coming of Secretariat in his barn. In consequence, the next time out he raises the horse a prohibitive degree in class and his would-be Secretariat winds up a nice snappy last.

So, to this degree, form and its relationship to class must be considered. This means that once one determines that current peak or near-peak racing condition is present, the next step is to determine if the animal is reasonably placed, i.e., competitive. But, for the moment let's concern ourselves with how a form cycle can be interpreted.

How to Analyze a Form Cycle

There's many clues, but unfortunately none are clean cut due to the multitude of variables that are usually involved. Some factors narrow down to requiring simple observation.

Example: A sprinter's recent races have been mediocre, then in its last race, for the first time, within the block of 10 races usually shown in the Daily Racing Form's past performance records, it manifests early speed up until the half-mile pole. At this point it appears to tire and winds up maybe sixth in a 10-horse field. This early speed would be a clue that the animal is rounding into form.

Another case might involve a router who after a siege of ho-hum efforts suddenly, in its most recent race, demonstrates a a sudden surge that moves it from ninth place, 10 lengths off the leader, to 4th place at the the finish, only three lengths behind the winner.

A third clue would be to watch for gradual improvement in a thoroughbred's performance by using beaten lengths as a criterion. Assume that in its third race back (using, as always, the Daily Racing Form's past performances for reference) a horse was 12 lengths off the winner at the finish. In its next outing it winds up only four lengths off, and in its last race loses by merely one length. This pyramid effect at the top of a past perfromance block can be a fine tipoff that the animal is nearing its peak.

These condition clues can work in reverse as well. Assume that a chronic early speed horse starts turning sluggish when braking from the gate. This should serve as a warning this its physical condition is tapering off. Or, a strong finisher, who usually exhibits a powerful surge of energy nearing the finish of a race, ceases making up ground in the stretch run. This too might indicate a staling off.

A current fad among selectors is termed **trip handicapping**. This involves an effort to pin point those horses that ran into difficulty in their last race. Maybe they went wide around a turn, were jostled, got off to a poor start, or met with any one of numerous mishaps that could and do occur during the running of a race. Trip handicappers usually use the track's video replay booths to request that they be allowed to view the tape of any specific race in which they have an interest.

My suggestion is that the same information and maybe even more can be gleaned by studying the past performance "running lines" of any race. This is less time consuming and probably a more efficient way to engage in trip handicapping.

What one should look for is erratic races. Assume that Horse C at the quarter pole was running third, two lengths off the leader. At the half-mile pole it's sixth, seven lengths off the horse in front. Then, at the finish it's fourth but only two lengths behind the winner. This falling back and the making up of ground with a strong finish would imply how the horse performed during the course of a race.

Typical of such comments, given at the end of each race's past performance line, would be, "No threat," "Gave way," "Went wide," "Outrun," "Strong finish," "Showed little," etc.

In addition, one can review a race in greater detail by carefully reading the chart maker's comments which accompany the racing charts of each day's races.

Permit me to emphasize an important point that I'll be repeating in one form or another all through the course of this writing. It's imperative that the reader should grasp it, and abide by it's principle.

Don't assume that any single aspect of handicapping will provide the answer to all handicapping problems. Many players tend to replace previous information with whatever recent information they may have gained. This is a mistake and voids any chance that one might have to improve his winner-selecting capability.

In a paragraph above we spoke of trip handicappers in a slightly deprecatory manner. However, we would imply the same tone if we were discussing speed handicappers or class handicappers - players who concentrate on seeking exacta tipoffs - or any type of player whose focus is solely on one aspect of handicapping to the exclusion of all others. Racing is far too broad in scope to enable any isolated narrow approach to succeed. What one's handicapping arsenal really requires is the intelligent use of all of these weapons combined.

The Weight Fallacy

Weight either on or off is the basis used by the track secretary when he endeavors to give every entry a chance to win in handicap races. The best horse carries top weight, and those of lesser quality are burdened with lower-weight packages.

In other types of races, such as allowance affairs, weight penalties and weight reductions are either imposed for recent good performance, or reduced for non-performance. An actual condition for an allowance type race is given below.

Allowance Race

3rd Race - Golden Spike   One Mile and a Furlong
**Purse $29,000. For Fillies and Mares Three Years Old and Upward which
have never won a race other than Maiden, Claiming or Starter.**
Three-Year-Olds.....120 lbs.   Older.....122 lbs.
Non-Winners of a race other than claiming at a mile
or over since November 1 allowed .....   3 lbs.
Of such a race since October 15   .....   5 lbs.

Let's see how this business of added weight is managed. Assume that a jockey weighs 112 pounds and the impost assigned is 118 pounds. The six pound difference would be made up by adding lead to a pocket in the horse's saddle. Horsemen generally are of the belief that "live weight" is easier on a horse than the dead weight represented by lead. For this reason they prefer to use a jockey whose actual weight comes as close to the assigned weight as possible.

Despite the almost universal belief among horsemen that weight is a major influence in the outcome of a race, there's an imposing array of arguments designed to refute this. An interesting sidelight is the fact that to this scribe's knowledge there has never been scientific proof that two, three or even 10 pounds on or off a thoroughbred's back will affect its performance to an appreciable degree!

This fact in itself is amazing when one considers that the multi-billion dollar thoroughbred racing and breeding industry should have a vital interest in substantiating to what degree weight affects performance. After all, weight-carrying ability, is one of the foundation stones upon which racing is built. One could reasonably assume that scientists, capable of conceiving the hydrogen bomb, and proving that the moon is not made of green cheese, would have little trouble devising a means to accurately assess weight's affect.

It is this writer's opinion, which he has expressed many times, that physical condition will influence a horse's performance far more than the impost it is obliged to carry.

Look at it from the following perspective. Horse A wins several successive handicap races. Each victory is accompanied by weight being added the next time it races. Let's assume that going into its fourth race, after three successive victories, that the track secretary-handicapper has assigned three additional pounds to the 118 that the animal last carried. Horse A loses to a lesser equine, and we again hear the ubiquitous refrain that weight is the great leveler. We fail to see the situation in that light.

Horses maintain top condition for only so long. Peak form cycles of the lesser animals might last for only a week or two, whereas a top grade thoroughbred might well maintain his form for a couple of months. The higher the class of horse, the longer it will tend to hold it's good racing condition. This is why the cheaper animals are noted for being erratic.

The fact, however, is that they all eventually stale off. A scenario for one animal might be that it first evinces evidence of approaching peak form by showing early speed and then appearing to tire before the finish line. Next time out though it holds its speed to the wire. It has now achieved its best or near-best racing form.

If our equine hero is a handicap performer, the track handicapper will assign it more weight for its next foray, and will continue adding a weight penalty after each successive win. Eventually the horse begins to stale off and embarks on the downgrade of its form cycle. It then loses and, as suggested, most interested spectators will attribute the loss to the weight it was obliged to carry. The actuality probably is that its loss was inevitable and would have occurred regardless of whatever impost was involved.

We're assuming of course that we're discussing a weight-imposed variance of from one to 20 pounds which is within the usual bounds.

Many times when a horse unseats its rider at the start of a race, the animal, responding to a reflex, will continue to race on its own and frequently forge to the front of the pack. This bit of drama leads some spectators to surmise that the horse would have won had it not been for the mishap. This is fallacious reasoning. Who could question that discharging 110 pounds of weight could indeed affect performance.

Our argument is limited to the assumption that far less poundage is involved and that a usual variance of anywhere from two to eight pounds, relative to the animal's approximate 1,000 pounds of solid muscle, will have very little effect.

This we feel is so, particularly when the total weight package is live weight that the jockey takes pains to balance over the animal's withers which tends to provide far less strain for the horse than if the full weight was sitting on its back.

It might seem that we deliberately glossed over the average of 110 to 114 pounds that the rider weighs, and only considered the weight differential of a few pounds. This was not the case. We discussed only the weight variance from one race to the next because the jockey's weight is an influence that's exerted on all the contestants and therefore balances itself out.

However, the fact remains that most horsemen do place considerable emphasis on the weight factor, and I'm sure that if a horse's form cycle has peaked, and it's now on the downgrade, that whatever added weight it has to carry will probably help the process along. On the other hand, when the animal is on the upgrade I would question severely the degree of influence that two or three pounds additional is going to make.

Handicap races provide a fine criterion for judging weight's influence. In such races the track handicapper assigns weight with the deliberate intent of giving every horse a fair chance. In theory, the idea is that the weights should be so equitably proportioned that all the contenders will finish in a dead heat to win.

To our knowledge, the closest that a major handicap ever came to achieving this ideal was in New York's Carter Handicap a number of years back. Three horses, Brownie, Bossuet and Wait A Bit defied the photo finish camera's ability to separate them at the finish line, and the race was declared a 3-way dead heat. Bars and Grills all over the Country have been flaunting an enlarged reproduction of this event ever since.

The point we really wish to emphasize, however, is that weight does *not* bring them all together. In handicap races the overwhelming trend is that the higher-weighted horses (not necessarily the TOP weighted) will monopolize the purse monies, and the low weights will rarely get more than the exercise.

Weight and Claimers

We've noted that control over claimers is exerted primarily in two ways:

1. Through use of the claiming box which subjects any horse to the threat of being claimed and.

2. Via use of weight, either on or off.

However, a weight disadvantage, regardless of its degree of effectiveness, can be offset in claiming races via one or more of several devices. Also, keep in mind that a weight-off concession is usually granted for non-performance. Such concessions are helpful to the handicapper as they suggest that a horse is inferior to its competitors.

A weight reduction (benefit) can be achieved by a trainer if he reduces the claiming price of his horse according to the stipulations provided in the racing conditions of that particular race. For example; if he enters the animal at the lowest claiming price as against the highest.

An additional device for seeking a weight advantage is to use an apprentice rider. As suggested by the description, an apprentice is a rider who has not yet reached the status of **journeyman**, or full-fledged rider.

To encourage horsemen to use the services of these relatively inexperienced riders certain weight concessions are granted. A **three bug apprentice** gets a 10 pound allowance until he or she has ridden five winners. A **two bug** boy gets a five pound weight concession until he achieves 30 winners.

However, if he has ridden 35 winners prior to the end of one year from the date of his fifth winner he shall have an allowance of five pounds until the end of that year.

After the completion of the foregoing conditions he may claim three pounds when riding horses owned or trained by his original contract employer assuming no change in contract ownership has taken place.

The above rules, somewhat paraphrased, are in accordance with the official Rules of Racing. We see then that the claiming trainer has a bit of latitude in controlling weight assignments. This suggests an important point. Regardless of the real or illusionary effect that weight might or might not have on a horse's performance, the fact remains that horsemen, generally, subscribe to the theory that weight is a major influence.

The alert player can frequently benefit from this near-universal belief of horsemen by noting which horses in a race appear to be placed most advantageously relative to weight. Keep in mind that it is the trainer's responsibility to see that his horse is properly weighted. If it is under-weighted the trainer is penalized.

On the other hand, it is not unusual to spot a horse in a race that has not received the full weight-off benefit to which it was entitled. The trainer appears to have been careless, and did not take advantage of the weight-off allowed (we'll assume), for using an apprentice, or he may have failed to take a benefit for non-performance as per the race's specifications. This means that the horse is penalized unnecessarily.

The interpretation of such carelessness on a conditioner's part can reasonably be construed to suggest he's not particularly interested in winning the race. He may regard it as simply a workout for his charge.

On the other hand, if it's noted that every conceivable weight advantage has been taken, it would then behoove the player to examine the animal's winning potential more closely.

A case in point: Horse A is entered in a top and bottom claiming race for the bottom price of $30,000, and thus gets a five pound allowance. The trainer last out used a journeyman, but today a hot apprentice has the leg up. This is another five pounds off.

The last race was on a fast track and Horse A, a good mudder, carried top weight and ran nowhere. Today it's confronted with an "off" track and gets in against the same band of horseflesh, but carrying 10 pounds less.

It should be obvious from such a scenario that the trainer at least believes he's got a shot at the purse. In such situations it would be up to the handicapper to decide whether or not to go along.

However, if the would-be handicapper is not well enough informed to recognize such clues then he ceases to be in a position to avail himself of this option.

We have never researched off-track races specifically, but our strong impression, based on years of observation, is that lightly-weighted horses seem to fare better under such conditions than when racing on fast tracks.

In effect, we're suggesting that weight concessions might be of greater importance on heavy, slow or otherwise binding surfaces. Apprentices, for example, seem to win more frequently when off-track surfaces prevail.

Consistency and Class

Unfortunately or otherwise, it is difficult to classify horses precisely. One cannot state correctly that Y is a low-grade claiming horse, and Z is an allowance horse, therefore Z is superior. The fact is that many categories overlap. Horses can and do migrate back and forth from one group to another.

It would be misleading to use the various categories such as claimers, allowances, handicaps, etc, as a means to classify horses. It is also not advisable to use purses alone for classification purposes. Currently, for example, in New York, a $75,000 claiming, route race has the same $31,000 purse value as an A2 sprint affair. (Allowance for non-winners of two other than maiden or claimer.)

Additionally, we mentioned previously that the age factor plays a big part in dictating the true class of a race. An A1 race for 2-year-olds tends to be vastly superior to a race with similar conditions for 4-year-olds and up. This is so despite the fact that purse values are the same.

To further complicate matters, a race restricted to local breds will have the same purse value as a similarly conditioned "open company" race, yet the local breds will usually be of lesser quality.

This tendency to simplify the class problem by using claiming prices and convenient catch-all labels can lead to costly misconceptions on the player's part.

Whenever a more capable trainer claims a horse and then moves it up to win, one will hear remarks such as "Ah ha! They're at again," or "See! They're using the juice."

The not-so subtle implication, of course, is that skulduggery was afoot. The fact, however is that, more often than not, the move-up and accompanying win were parts of a logical sequence that exemplified nothing more heinous than the application of good horse-wise common sense.

To illustrate: Trainer X has his halterman's eye focused on a 6-year-old gelding who is a multi-winner in claiming races, and is now running for a $14,000 claiming tag. The animal in the past has demonstrated a degree of class, and its record attests to the fact that it has a will to win. Trainer X is aware that the gelding has physical problems but is confident they're ones he can cope with. He's checked the condition book and found that there's an "allowance one" race coming up that designates "for 4-year-olds and up."

Trainer X correctly foresees that this race will probably attract mediocrities who in all probability have succeeded in winning only one lone race in several years of competition, and that race was against maidens. They are running in an allowance race only because their owners are reluctant to risk losing them in a claiming race.

Why? Who knows! In any case, X makes his claim. He then enters it in this allowance race and wins at a 4-figure mutuel. Any knowledgeable fan, not fooled by labels, could easily have had this winner. Yet, in such cases, aspersions that assault the character of a trainer will abound.

This is as good a spot as any to interject the comment that what many or even most trainers look for when contemplating a claim, is the type horse that usually manages to bring home some portion of a purse whenever they run. In other words the ideal is to find a consistent animal that possesses a competitive spirit.

This concept of seeking **consistency** in a horse's performance is an important ingredient of good handicapping. It is as valid an approach for the selector as it is for the horseman. Many years ago, during the Forties, a lawyer named Robert Saunders Dowst built quite a reputation for himself for with a handicapping book titled, "*Win, Place and Show* ," and a series of articles in the prestigious men's magazine, *Esquire.*

Dowst made quite a case for consistency being of major importance in the handicapping of horses. Logically, he had a point. If a horse cannot be relied on to run back to a previous performance, or performances, the smartest handicapping in the world will achieve nothing.

Currently one reads and hears much about trip handicapping, pace handicapping, speed figures, trainer handicapping, computerized handicapping, etc., but rarely if ever does one see or hear mention of consistency as being a central or even an important ingredient of sound handicapping.

Our suggestion: Give consistency its proper emphasis.

13. BETTING OPTIONS

Each race presents the fan with an opportunity to decide what would be the most intelligent way to bet the particular race in question. His varied decisions can be important.

Not too long ago the racing fan had only four betting options. He could make a win, place, or show bet, and was permitted to wager on a Daily Double involving the first two races.

That was it.

Currently he is confronted with a much greater array. On a normal day, he may be offered win, place and show betting; two daily double bets; nine exactas; two quinellas; a triple and a Pick Six. To some fans this plethora of wagering opportunity can seem overwhelming. Let's try to avoid this feeling by subjecting each type of bet to close scrutiny.

We strongly suggest that the player abide rigidly by one rule:

Never get on a line to make a wager before you know exactly how, and which horse you are going to bet.

This means that if you are undecided about a race simply pass the race. There's no law saying you must bet. A common error is for a fan to remain undecided until he's actually at the betting window and then suddenly, on impulse, he makes a wager. Avoid doing this. It can prove costly.

Study each race carefully; horse by horse. Know in advance positively what your bet will be so that when a race is over you won't feel you overlooked something, or be one of those who go around lamenting, "I was gonna bet that horse but changed my mind." To paraphrase an erstwhile popular expression, "Betting should mean never having to say you're sorry." After any race one will hear disgruntled bettors bemoaning the fact that they should have done this, or should have done that. Don't be one of those shoulda, coulda, woulda people. Be among the few who actually do.

Win, Place and Show Betting

If one makes a bet for win, place or show it is called **straight betting**. Most fans ignore the show hole because of its relatively insignificant payoffs. However, there are occasions when the ultra-conservative individual who is a big bettor finds it prudent to give this spot consideration.

The natural trend is that the lower the odds are on a horse the greater becomes the likelihood that it will be an overlay in the third spot. Going to extremes to make the point; there's many an occasion wherein a heavily favored horse at odds of say 2/5 to win will pay $2.40 for show.

What this means is that the win payoff was $2.80 whereas the show payoff was a disproportionately high 50% of the win price. It is disproportionately high simply because the win spot offers only one opportunity to cash a ticket - the horse must win.

In contrast the show spot offers THREE chances. The show bettor cashes his ticket regardless of whether the horse runs first, second or third. Therefore, it follows that if one's chance improves three fold the return should decrease three fold, and thus be only one third of the win payoff.

In this example, a proportionately correct show-bet return would equal one third of the win return. This translates into a theoretical mutuel payoff of $2.27 ($0.133 is one third of $0.40).

Understanding the foregoing detail is not too important. What is important is to understand the principle involved; which is that the lower the win odds are, the greater becomes the likelihood of there being an overlay in either or both the place or show slots. The opposite of this also prevails. The longer the odds are the less attractive play becomes anywhere except on the win end.

Let me be more explicit. Low odds suggest that a horse should be bet to place (forget about show betting unless you are one of the heavy hitters). Contrarily, the longer the odds the greater the incentive to bet it strictly on the win end. This is so because place and show bets on horses other than favorites tend to be disproportionately small. The longer the odds the more this applies.

Example: A favorite that pays a mutuel of $5.00 ($1.50 to $1.00) frequently will pay $3.80 or more to place ($0.90 to $1.00). Obviously this is a relative bargain.

On the other hand, a selection that pays $12.00 to win (5/1 odds) will most likely pay $5.80 or less (9/5) to place. Ideally its place payoff should be $7.00 (2-1/2 to 1) or one half of its win price.

We see therefore that the place payoff is disproportionately low compared to the increased potential offered for cashing such a bet.

Our conclusion therefore is that when contemplating a straight bet on a choice held at low odds consideration should be given to betting it to place rather than to win.

But, if a longshot is the one under consideration the bet usually should be to win only.

SHORT AND LONG FIELDS

The following is the way that I handle my wagering activities when making straight bets.

First off, I tend to divide racing into two groups; those consisting of eight horses or less, and those composed of nine horses or more. My personal experience is that **short fields**, eight horses or less, contrary to what they might seem, are the toughest to beat. In consequence I approach them with added caution.

Short Fields

When dealing with fields of eight and less, particularly if the favorite is a short price (below the average of 8/5) I rarely make a place bet. The reason being that if I'm considering the favorite I usually decide that I'd be better off making an exacta bet using the favorite as my key.

On the other hand, if I incline toward any horse other than the favorite I would only consider a win bet unless the favorite was unusually long (5/2 or more). The reasoning here is that low and average priced favorites in short fields run second approximately 64% of the time, and whenever the favorite runs in with another choice it literally ruins the place payoff of that choice.

Example: Assume that a favorite monopolizes 50% of the place pool and runs either first or second. The "choice" that was selected over the favorite has only 10% of the place pool wagered on it. If it also has 10% of the win pool this means that, after the track's take has been allowed for, it is held at win odds of 7/1.

Therefore in order for it to be equitable it should have the potential of paying 3-1/2 to 1 for place. Let's see what its prospects actually are.

Assume that there's $1,000 total to be paid out in the place pool. The favorite and the 7/1 shot will split evenly whatever winnings are involved. To determine the winnings we first must deduct the total amounts bet on the two horses. This comes to $600.00; $500.00 (50%) representing the favorite and $100.00 (10%) representing the 7/1 shot. We see then that there's $400.00 left to be shared.

The $500.00 bet on the favorite will return a total of $700.00 to its backers which equals a mutuel payoff of $2.80 or 40¢ profit for every dollar wagered. This is a huge (but by no means rare) bargain considering that after deductions for take and breakage, the win payoff would only be $3.20.

The backers of the 7/1 horse also have winnings of $200.00 which means that their mutuel place tickets will be $6.00 ($200.00 to pay off $100.00 equals odds of 2/1).

From this example you can see to what degree the favorite decimated the place payoff on the animal that had the misfortune of running in with it. An arithmetically correct place payoff would be $9.00 (3-1/2 to 1) but its supporters received only $6.00; 57% below the winnings they were entitled to.

Long Fields

In fields of nine and more, **long fields**, the consequence of having a favorite run in with another horse is somewhat lessened, but still should be subject to careful consideration before deciding the best way to bet.

Low Odds - Bet to Place

Horses at 9/2 or less should be considered as prospects for place betting, providing they are not in races with relatively short-priced favorites (8/5 or less). However, when making place bets avoid the booby trap of growing careless with your handicapping. Too often the place bettor will settle for a horse with "a good chance to run second."

Don't do this. Even though you are making a place bet do it only when you think the horse is strong enough to be the logical winner.

One major reason to give place betting serious consideration is it can help avoid the demoralizing effect of running into that occasional, extended run of losers that is inevitable when betting is confined to the win end.

Despite the overall high win average of favorites, they still have been known to lose 30 and more consecutive races. The implication to this is that any group of selections can occasionally hit a disaster area. I've observed over the years that my bad streaks seem synchronized with **off** tracks. In consequence I approach races which are run in mud, or slop with considerable caution.

To illustrate the value of place betting: Let us assume that the record of a certain newspaper handicapper (despite his good overall performance) shows that within the last year he had one terrible streak of 27 straight losers. This same record might well indicate that if these 27 horses had been bet to place, rather than to win, the longest string of consecutive losses would have been confined to merely six.

The gist of what we're saying is that short-priced horses (9/2 or less) should be considered for place betting inasmuch as their payoffs quite often are within acceptable bounds. This applies providing they are not obliged to compete against heavily-backed favorites.

The line of demarcation indicating such favorites is 8/5 (or less). Also, we're saying that place betting helps to avoid extended runs of losing bets which not only deflate one's bankroll, but can produce a most undesirable demoralizing affect that will have a negative impact on one's judgement.

High Odds: Bet to Win

What does one do about a horse whose odds are 5/1 or more? The rule of thumb is, bet it to win. However, if one has developed a penchant for place betting along with its accompanying feeling of security, there's a sensible way to bet such horses to place even when you recognize that the favorite could lower your potential payoff.

Example: An 8-horse field is being considered. The favorite is a so-so 9/5 and seems far from being a shoo-in. However, statistically speaking, he does stand at least a 50/50 chance of running second or better. In this same race you like a 6/1 shot that looms a cinch to be no worse than second.

You'd like to make a substantial place bet, but you're aware that if your choice runs in with the favorite you'll take a beating on the price. What to do?

The Exacta Box

Here's the solution I've worked out. In effect, I buy insurance. I do this by first betting the 6/1 horse to place. Let's assume I bet $50. I then invest another $6.00 and buy a $3.00 exacta box consisting of the favorite tied in with the 6/1 shot.

A **box** means that two exacta bets were made on one ticket. One bow is bet calling for the favorite to win and the other horse to run second. The second exacta requires that the opposite finish should prevail.

The reasoning behind this particular exacta box is that if the favorite runs worse than second the place payoff will be generous enough to more than compensate for the lost $6 exacta "insurance bet." On the other hand, if the favorite wins, and I get second, the resulting exacta payoff will suffice to far and away compensate for the shortened place price.

But, the ideal situation would be if the 6/1 horse won and the favorite ran second. The exacta would then be substantial, and I'd still collect on the place end. The amount of the exacta bet you make should be whatever you, as the bettor, consider to be in reasonable proportion to the place bet made.

For example: If you bet $10 to place then you might decide that a $1 box (at a cost of $2) would suffice as insurance.

Favorites, in most cases should be bet to place as opposed to straight win betting. We're not saying that all favorites should automatically be bet to place. We're saying that if you like a favorite then, generally speaking, the best way to wager on it is in the place hole.

Exacta Betting

My experience is that exacta betting should be regarded as a useful investment tool. With practically every race offering the option of exacta betting, along with several other choices, one should ask themselves prior to each race, "What is the most sensible way for me to wager in this particular instance?"

Subject your contemplated bet to close scrutiny and ask yourself, "Will this provide the best possible value in this particular race?"

Previously we offered one example wherein an exacta served the useful function of providing insurance. Another situation that will frequently be confronted presents the dilemma of whether to make a place bet or an exacta bet.

Example: A race is made up of a field of 10 horses. The favorite is a slightly high 2/1, and you like one of the contenders held at 9/2, Should you make a place bet or should you use the 9/2 horse as a key in the exacta?

My inclination would be to make a place bet. Whether the favorite runs in with it or not, the place payoff will be relatively healthy. Plus - and this is the major contribution to my reasoning — there's nothing else in the race that I feel offers genuine competition. Therefore, there's little incentive to tie the 9/2 shot in with anything else.

It is this scribe's strong opinion that exactas should never be played without a **key** (strong) horse being involved. A common failing is for a player to create a three horse box which in effect is six individual exactas. They think that no matter which of the three might run 1-2 the player will collect. That part's great. The not-so great part is when they don't run 1-2 and six bets go down the drain in one fell swoop.

This blunderbuss type of wagering can prove very expensive and deflate a bankroll faster than one can say, "Gee whiz, I'm broke". It can't represent a good bet because by implication it states that the bettor has no strong preference in the race, and is merely hoping to get lucky.

This is sheer gambling as opposed to thoughtful investing. If a race is so competitive that three or more horses present themselves as equal possibilities you're better off to simply pass the race.

Exacta boxes should be confined to those races wherein you're convinced that your selection should win, but at the least be no worse than second. However, you can see where two or three of the public's secondary choices will probably present the real opposition.

The betting in such an instance might look somewhat like the following (no attention has been paid to making a proper book):

1	2/1
2	5/2
3	4/1
4	9/2 (your choice)
- and the balance of the field is held at 7/1 or higher	

The 9/2 is your key horse. It is suggested that in such cases it's advisable to buy either two or three exacta boxes.

Don't try to handicap for a second horse. It's difficult enough to select one horse to win (your key horse), without trying to pick 'em one-two. Instead of handicapping for a second horse use your knowledge of racing percentages and hook your selection up with horses 1 and 2, or 1, 2 and 3 shown above.

The reasoning behind this maneuver is that the three horses you've used as possibilities to run in with your selection, are perfectly logical inasmuch as they represent a combined chance of about 80% to run either first or second.

Assume you have the choice of making either a $20.00 place bet OR buying three $2.00 exacta boxes. I would reason that a place bet probably would pay a maximum of $6.00 (2/1), whereas a successful exacta could return as much as $60.00, or more. This offers the potential of getting 4/1 odds ($48.00 winnings on a $12.00 wager) or double the potential offered by a place bet.

In such cases I would figure that an 80% chance to double the odds warrants the additional risk involved.

Also, if your 9/2 goodthing should have the poor taste to NOT run either first or second you're still ahead because you saved eight dollars.

Quinellas

A Quinella provides the player with a choice. He can combine two horses in an Exacta or use the same two horses in a **Quinella**. The difference is that with an Exacta, if he wants to be assured that he'll cash regardless of which of his two horses win, with the other running second, he's obligated to box the two selections. This, in effect means buying two tickets.

The advantage to the Quinella is that the same objective is accomplished when purchasing only one ticket (meaning it cost only half as much as an exacta). The catch is that there's a payoff differential. In theory, if the fact that the Quinella costs only half as much as the Exacta, it should pay only half as much.

In actual practice, however, the Quinella quite often will pay considerably more than 50% of the Exacta in the same race. The player who contemplates an Exacta in a race offering Quinella betting would be well advised to check the monitors that show potential payoffs for both prior to the running of the race and before deciding how to bet.

Let's assume a bettor likes Horse A and Horse B. He's considering a $2.00 Exacta box which would cost $4.00. Checking the monitor just prior to post time he sees that an Exacta would pay $40.00, but a Quinella on the same two horses would pay $26.00.

What would be the sensible thing to do?

Obviously the proper bet would be to buy two $2.00 Quinella tickets due to the fact that for the same $4.00 risk there's a prospective return of $52.00 as against only $40.00 from an Exacta box.

This is a 30% greater return. This is by no means an unusual occurrence.

Daily Doubles

In New York there is the standard **early double** composed of the first and second races. Then there is the **late double** made up of the eighth and ninth race each day. On occasion there are doubles offered in-between. These come about due to some races having only five or less betting units which precludes exacta betting. In such cases there's an "instant" double created which consists of the short-field event and the race that follows.

The major point that one should understand is that - unequivocally - the DD offers the fan the greatest bargain in racing. This is due to the fact that Daily Doubles have their own separate betting pool. In consequence this means that one can play two races (by combining his or her selections and betting the double) with only ONE take and breakage deducted.

If the same two horses were bet individually there would be two deductions of about 19% apiece. Therefore, in effect a DD bet reduces the nut by 50%.

Also, considering the advantage that the DD enjoys, we grew curious as to how a series of DD bets would shape up in comparison with parlay betting. Many race writers have called attention to the fact that the DD is a bargain, but I know of none who offered **Proof**.

We decided to remedy the situation. The way we went about

it was to use parlay betting as our control. We compared DD payoffs to what the same horses would have paid if played as parlays.

After checking more than 200 such situations the conclusion was that overall DDs pay about 5% more than the same combinations would have produced if bet as parlays. However, there's more to it than that. The same survey indicated that the greatest advantage occurs when relatively low-priced horses are involved, and diminishes as the odds increase.

Roughly 66% of our DDs paid substantially more than a parlay, and among the other 34% we observed that at least one horse was a longshot.

A prime example, illustrating what happens when longshots are involved, was a case wherein the DD paid $978.00 but a parlay on the same two horses would have netted $1,159.00. This was an 18.5% higher return. Our conclusion therefore is that DDs generally are good bets, but are even better when both choices are 5/1 or less.

Such winning DDs tend to offer a far greater advantage over parlays than the mere 5% for ALL DDs would indicate.

Here is an example serving to demonstrate the considerable benefit that a DD offers over a parlay when FAVORITES are involved. One horse paid $2.80 to win. The other paid $6.60 (actual races). The daily double payoff was $12.60. A parlay would have returned $9.20 after allowing for breakage. This is a differential of 37% in favor of the DD.

OK! We agree that the DD is frequently a bargain. But, there's also another important benefit that it can provide.

The Early Double as a Control

My observation is that if a player incurs heavy losses early in a race day, the tendency is for his or her equilibrium to be upset, and for the individual's judgement to be impaired for the rest of the session. If this is so, it then follows that one should avoid this occurrence as much as it's within their power to do so. The following offers one possible solution to the problem.

Start off the day by making a modest Daily Double wager.

Assume that one is ordinarily a $20.00 bettor. Select choices in the first and second race and buy a two dollar ticket. Why? Because if your first selection runs out you've saved $18.00 and avoid the possibility of being influenced adversely by an early loss.

On the other hand, if your first horse wins you probably will have a substantial amount automatically riding on the second race. Then if both halves win your return will be reasonably gratifying. If the second half of the ticket loses, so what? You can afford to be philosophical.

You're now up to the third race with your finances, unlike that of most other attendees, still in good shape.

My personal preference is to buy two Daily Double tickets for whatever amount I might feel is prudent. I would make only one selection in the first race and use this as my key and tie it in with two selections in the second race.

Why this particular routine?

For no other reason than that it is reassuring to have two chances in the second half. It's as if the major obstacle has been surmounted. If this procedure were reversed (a key horse in the second race) it wouldn't be quite as reassuring.

It is suggested that the late double (or any other) be approached from the simple perspective that it and they are bargains and should be played in preference to betting the individual races involved. The advantages have already been discussed.

The Pick-Six and Triples

We now have only **Triples**, and **Pick-Six** type bets to be considered. We disapprove of both bets on principle due to the extortionary tax of about 27%. Plus, if you should get lucky and hit a good payoff, the government takes still another 20%. The entire concept is ridiculous.

But if the triple must be played, approach it only when you have a strong key horse. Don't tie up a lot of money in all sorts of combinations. Keep in mind that every time you make another bet in the same race you are reducing your odds. Assume that with one ticket for $2.00 the prospective payoff is $202.00 or 100/1. If you vary the combination and buy two tickets you have now reduced your odds to 50/1.

In any case, there's nothing wrong with occasionally stabbing at either a triple or a Pick Six as long as you don't go overboard. Relative to the triple, I suggest using a key on the win end and buying two tickets as follows: Key with 1 and 2, and Key with 2 and 1. My further suggestion is to make this the extent of your triple gambling.

As for the Pick Six, if you feel lucky, bet it, but keep your wagers down. My occasional play is for $8.00. I use two horses in the third race and two in the eighth race (the first and last races in the Pick Six).

The first time I did this, the Pick Six was relatively new, and I wasn't familiar with this form of wagering. I got lucky and tabbed the first five winners, but blew the final race. The Pick Five "consolation" payoff was $538.00 which I felt gratified to be receiving. I turned in my $8.00 ticket and was startled to receive $1,076.00 back; twice the sum I expected.

Knowing it was unlikely that the machines made an error, I left the window more than a bit puzzled, and sat down to think it over.

Finally I realized that my single $8.00 ticket was actually four $2.00 tickets and two of the four tickets had hit the Pick Five.

Here is how I originally wrote the ticket:

Race 1	Horse
1	1 and 2
2	3
3	4
4	5
5	6
6	7 and 8

These, of course, were not the actual numbers played, but are used to illustrate how my ticket looked. The breakdown showing the set-up of how the ticket was actually 4-in-1 follows:

```
1 1 2 2
3 3 3 3
4 4 4 4
5 5 5 5
6 6 6 6
7 8 7 8
```

Consequently, when my "1" horse won the first race and four more winners followed, it meant I had two winning Pick Fives. One can now understand why I'm partial to this approach on the rare occasions when I bet the Pick Six.

The Pick Three

While we were in the midst of laboring over this treatise, the New York Racing Association decided to introduce a new type of bet to Big Apple racing fans: **The Pick Three**.

At this point we've had no direct experience with this form of wagering, but from what we've learned, and as near as we can judge, this would appear to be one of the good guys among NYRA's various betting mediums. The reasons why the Pick Three would appear to be a desirable option are:

1. Similar to the Daily Double pool, there will be only one take-out inasmuch as this betting mode involves a separate pool. This means that the bettor can play three races and be penalized with 25% take-out only one time: A big advantage.

2. A dollar minimum bet will be permitted as opposed to the Pick Six requiring a $2.00 minimum bet. The advantage here is two-fold;

a. The fan is afforded an opportunity to play a number of combinations without the total bet assuming the proportions of the National debt;

b. A winning ticket will be less likely to be subjected to the Federal and State on-the-spot tax deduction.

3. Inasmuch as this bet involves the fifth, sixth and seventh races, the overall quality of the races should be relatively better than the card as a whole. The second and fourth races in New York are frequently the ones least subject to analytical handicapping.

4. Unlike the early Daily Double which consists of race one and two, the fact that the betting will start at the fifth race implies that there will be proportionately better (larger) payouts. The reason?

Because at the beginning of the day the public tends to be conservative, but as the day progresses, and take and breakage extracts its inevitable toll, the public grows less selective and more inclined toward stabbing, as opposed to rational selecting.

5. The complete pool will be paid out every day, unlike the Pick Six wherein if there is no winner, 75% of the pool gets held over to the following day.

All in all, the Pick Three wager appeals to us as a reasonably good investment option.

We've now pretty well covered the broad spectrum of racing, and will utilize the balance of this tome to concentrate on statistical data that should serve to both increase one's defense and improve his offense in the on-going war with racing's **iron men**, otherwise known as the parimutuel machines.

14. WINNING PERCENTAGES BY BETTING POSITION

Years ago when take and breakage combined amounted to about 11%, this writer got involved in a survey of 10,466 races that established the fact that play on all favorites produced a flat-bet loss of 10.3%. Second choices lost 13.8%, and third choices sustained a loss of about 15.6%.

This analysis was continued right on down the line to the 12th choice and demonstrated that the percentage of losses increased in direct ratio to the betting position. That is to say that the fifth choice showed greater losses than the fourth; the sixth more than the fifth, and so on.

Additionally, favorites won 32.6% of all races. Second choices won 19.9% of the time, and third choices scored in 14.4% of their races. Combined, the top three choices accounted for 66.9% of all wins. Since that project other surveys have frequently offered similar figures.

However, "The times they are a'changin'."

In the era of the original analysis, the take and breakage was considerably less than it is today, and the current fevered trend toward emphasizing computerized handicapping, and exotic bets had not yet burst into full flower. These factors have greatly affected previously established standards.

Two major influences exist nationally. A 17% takeout is practically universal, and in today's frenetic gambling climate no racing center could survive without offering high-risk, high-return exotic betting. Another influence also exists; race-players are increasingly subscribing to and using hi-tech handicapping services along with computer generated information.

The following statistics are designed to bring these standards up-to-date.

ROWE'S 2,317 RACE SURVEY

This current survey, encompassing 2,317 consecutive races is the first one, to our knowledge, that takes the above-mentioned three influences into consideration, and provides more than sufficient volume to insure that the data is not a statistical aberration.

Let's begin with a review of how the top three choices fared overall. The clearest way to present this will be in table form. We'll use the same format throughout.

Top Three Choices to Win
(Favorites, 2nd & 3rd Choices)

> ### Favorites to Win
> 773 wins/2,317 races equal 33.6%
> X $2.00
> $4,634.00 **invested** $3,790.70 **returned**
> $843.30 **loss** (-18.2%)

We see from this that favorites won 773 out of 2,317 races or 33.6% of the times. This is slightly more than one out of every three races. On a $2.00 flat-bet basis we invested $4,634.00 and the return was $3,790.70 equalling a loss of $843.30 or 18.2%. Let's see how they fared in the place hole.

> ### Favorites to Place
> 1,258 placed/2,317 races equalling 54.3%
> X $2.00
> $4,634.00 **invested** $4,062.00 **returned**
> $572.00 **loss** (-12.3%)

From this it should be apparent that favorites to place are far and away the preferred spot. Not only are more bets cashed, which is good for one's morale, but the overall loss is far less than that which applies on the win end. Let's move now to second choices and see how they compare.

Second Choices to Win
486 wins/2,317 races equalling 21%
X $2.00
$4,634.00 **invested** $893.60 **returned**
$740.40 **loss** (-16%)

Second Choices to Place
907 placed/2,317 races equalling 39.1%
X $2.00
$4,634.00 **invested** $3,906.20 **returned**
$727.80 **loss** (-15.7%)

We next come to third choices.

Third Choices to Win
363 wins/23l7 races equalling 15.7%
X $2.00
$4,634.00 **invested** $3,902.20 **returned**
$ 731.80 **loss** (-15.8%)

Third Choices to Place
738 placed/2317 races equalling 31.9%
X $2.00
$4,634.00 **invested** $3,795.20 **returned**
$838.80 **loss** (-18.1%)

Current Survey (Winning Percentage)

Now we'll compare the results of our earlier survey with the current one. The first table shows winning percentages in each category, and the second, the percentage of loss that each category produced.

Win Result	1st Survey	2nd Survey
Favorite	32.6%	33.6%
Second Choice	19.9%	21.0%
Third Choice	14.4%	15.7%

Note how in each case the winning percentage INCREASED. This appears to be more than coincidence. Let's now look at the dollar percentage of loss that was produced by each of the top three choices.

Win Result	1st Survey	2nd Survey
Favorite	-10.3%	-18.2%
Second Choice	-13.8%	-15.0 %
Third Choice	-15.6%	-15.7%

Fixed Percentages by Betting Position

There are certain percentages that hold steady year-in and year out at every racetrack on the North American continent. Most prominent and reliable among these are the following:

1. Favorites will win approximately 33% of all races.

2. Second choices will win about 21% of all races.

3. Third choices will win about 14% of all races.

Additionally, favorites will place about 53% of the times. Second choices will run second approximately 42% of the times. Third choices manage to get second with about a 30% frequency rate. These figures are not immutable. They can and do vary quite a bit within the short range.

For example; at one race meeting the favorites might average only 28% winners, whereas another meeting might average 36%.

Regardless, at the end of any one year, if one consults an authoritive source, such as the *American Racing Manual,* he or she will see that favorites overall achieved their customary quota by winning approximately one race out of every three, and the second choice scored about once in every five tries, and so forth.

Now, we cannot over-emphasize the fact that these figures represent averages. They do not imply that the favorite will win one time out of every three consecutive races, or that the second choice will perform in like manner once in every five tries. What they do convey is that over the long haul the winning percentages tend to balance out.

15. SMART MONEY HANDICAPPING

The comparison in the previous chapter of Yesterday and Today - so to speak - is fascinating. Our viewpoint is that it provides an excellent criteria for judging just how well **smart money** does.

It would appear that today's punters, with the aid of their modems, computers, 900 numbers and costly sheets, are being helped with their handicapping to the degree that they are selecting more winners. At least this is so relative to the top two choices which provide the obvious areas for the concentration of heavy action.

In fact, many horses that originally were not first or second choices in the early betting are made so by post time due solely to the money sent in by the big bettors.

On the other hand, they've gained nothing. In fact, something has been lost. The very concentration of money on horses with an obvious edge (as pin-pointed by the various "aids" used by today's handicappers) tends to lower mutuel payoffs on these horses!

In racing parlance such horses become underlays, and tend to defeat the basic goal of getting value for one's betting money!

Maybe we're making this unnecessarily complicated. What we're saying in plain Americanese is that big-money bettors all tend to use similar hi-tech handicapping aids, and because of this their money invariably seems to migrate toward the same selection, and thereby becomes self-defeating.

At this point it seems advisable to lend support to the foregoing theory relative to the effect that big money has. Some readers might feel that we exaggerate this effect. The simple fact is that it is NOT exaggerated.

The present day situation with racing is somewhat akin to that which prevails on Wall Street. Computerized buy and sell signals provide stock brokers with information that suggests what action they should take. So many are influenced at the same time by the same buy and sell signals that it has become common for brokers to act in unison.

Thus, frenetic mass buying and mass selling can take place almost instantaneously causing market gyrations that make the Dow Jones chart look like a picture of Coney Island's scenic railway. This situation, in fact, is what led to the huge stock sell off in October 1987 and created a near panic.

A similar condition seems to exist with racing. A small group of affluent players use what are known as **The Sheets**, and/or subscribe to computerized data-base services.

The result is that these sheets, and the trend toward using computerized handicapping, have the effect, to a great degree, of focusing attention on one or two more or less obvious horses in many races. Therefore, even though in theory the users of such approaches should arrive at differing judgements, the fact is that many of them arrive at similar conclusions.

Because the selections themselves are sound, this trend toward hi-tech handicapping tends to maintain favorites at or above a winning level that has come to be accepted as normal, but because of the concentrated monetary volume it generates, it lowers the mutuel payoff.

All of which applies to the second choice as well because in most races the real contention lies between it and the favorite, and thus these are the ones that attract the heavy play; frequently dividing it.

Notice that our emphasis is on the win factor. This is because there's little concentration of hi-tech betting on the place end due to the option players have of being able to bet exactas and quinellas instead. Therefore, place payoffs over the years have remained relatively unaffected, and are in line with the increases in take and breakage which have taken place.

Summed up, we're saying that the big bettors, on average, pick only slightly more winners than the public generally, but because many of them frequently settle on the same horse their heavy play tends to create low win mutuels when compared to what historic payoffs have been.

Proof: Check back on our table showing **Favorites To Win**. You'll note that the gross return was $3,790.70. Divide this sum by the 773 winners attained and the resulting figure indicates that the average win mutuel approximated $4.90. In contrast, previous standards produced a figure of $5.49, which is about 12% higher than the current average. Place mutuels appear relatively unaffected.

How to Avoid Big Money Bets

In many major racing circuits, certain handicapping information is incorporated into what the cognoscente refer to as *The Sheets*. The information provided consists of the lifetime racing histories of any and every horse entered on any specific day.

This data endeavors to show, graphically, the form cycles and speed potential of each entrant. However, similar to the information contained in the *Daily Racing Form*, the data, in theory, is subject to each individual's interpretation. But, obviously, whenever one horse is indicated as being superior there will be a tendency for most users of the sheets to arrive at a similar conclusion and consequently settle on the same selection.

Be this as it may, the fact is that users of these sheets pay from $18.00 to $31.00 a day to purchase them. Two rival organizations offer similar information in New York. One stakes out its claim in the grandstands, and the other has the clubhouse as its exclusive domain.

Now, it can safely be concluded that anyone spending up to $9,300 per year for information is not a $2.00 bettor.

Therefore, based on the formidable cost it is reasonable to assume that sheet buyers are big bettors, and represent a huge segment of the loot that gets shovelled into the maw of the mutuels prior to each race. In fact, it's been estimated that this source (a mere handful of bettors) accounts for more than 55% of New York's total daily play.

However, disregarding exact percentages, it's obvious that the sheet users, along with those who subscribe to expensive computerized data base services, bet amounts that are sufficient to influence the final odds.

Back now to the question, how can we differentiate between normal betting and the betting of the heavy hitters? The approach devised enabling us to arrive at an answer was to use bet-down horses as the criteria. The assumption being that the relatively small group that places its faith in the sheets and/or automated information is responsible for most of the bet downs that occur.

Okay! We first had to establish what could be considered normal play.

For this purpose we used the first early-money line that offered sufficient volume to be meaningful. We regarded the favorite and the favorite's odds in this money line as representing the public's choice, and the public's estimate of what constituted proper odds when weighed against its actual winning chance.

The Three Types of Betting Action

We regard the general public as one of three groups that influence the odds. We next concluded that there are three types of betting action that can take place:

1. The final odds will fall below those established by our initial money line.
2. The final odds will remain approximately the same.
3. The final odds will be higher than that of the original money line.

We'll analyze No.2 first. This situation is one wherein a favorite all through the betting remains at just about the SAME odds as the initial money line indicated. It originally (we'll assume) was 9/5 and it closed at 9/5.

We interpret such cases as being 100% representative of the public's point of view. In this example the public encompasses every betting group inclusive of most handicappers, public selectors, big bettors, who were not betting big, and horsemen.

The favorite remained at the same odds because there was no strong influence that exerted a change, and the later monies that came in were in full agreement with the early action that took place. Usually the early action is predominantly from the $2 bettors, and from OTB.

We next look at No.3, a favorite that goes *up* in the odds, possibly from 8/5 to 9/5 or even 2/1 by post time. This situation is brought about because the public has lost a segment of its support.

This segment, as we see it, is made up of the racing community itself and includes shed row workers, mutuel clerks, horsemen, restaurant employees, etc. Money from this source usually comes in slowly and in small sums from the track workers, their wives, friends and so forth, but as a cumulative amount it exerts considerable influence.

The favorite chosen by the original bettors is simply not being subscribed to by track employees who tend to base their conclusions and betting actions more on "inside info" than on handicapping via past performances.

"Inside info" in this case is meant to convey that some word has circulated throughout the track. Maybe it concerns a super workout that wasn't made public, or an owner was said to have made a big wager, or whatever. Any such rumor circulates quickly and can set off strong betting action

On the other hand, track rumors can have a negative impact which would cause such "insiders" to lay off a favorite, or to concentrate their money on some other choice. This negative reaction by track personnel often produces a situation that causes a favorite's odds to rise by post time. Track personnel, as you can see, comprises the second group that we feel can influence the odds.

We now arrive at No.1 situation; a favorite (or a second choice) whose odds drop by post time. Big money almost invariably waits until a minute or two prior to post time before betting. Example: When a horse's odds move from 8/5 to 7/5 about two minutes before post it can safely be assumed that such movement was the result of the big bettors going into action. They make up our third group which is capable of influencing the odds.

Well, we've done our best to present the overall mutuel picture as it relates to our survey of the top three choices.

Let's now take a look at bet-downs, and see how we can benefit by them.

16. HOW TO ANALYZE BET-DOWNS

Go to any racetrack in the country and you'll observe hordes of racing fans who do little else except stand around watching the fluctuations in the odds as shown on either the track monitors or the infield tote board.

Inasmuch as such fans rarely seem to possess a *Daily Racing Form*, it's safe to assume that whatever information or misinformation they derive from their odds-board studying, it's the only criterion they use as a means of selection. Their goal is to determine which horse they are betting on. No one ever has explained who it is these people regard as the mysterious "they."

In recent years another group has formed that does little else but watch the specific monitors that are devoted to displaying what various exacta combinations will pay if successful. This group is no more than a variation of the first group, and they too seldom resort to the use of a *Racing Form* .

In the first instance the board watchers are looking for **play-downs** - horses that appear to be getting unusually large betting action in the win pool. In the second instance they are doing precisely the same thing except now they are looking for *pairs* of horses in the exacta pool that get what is interpreted as a disproportionate share of betting action.

The fact that there are so many of these "exacta checkers" leads me to believe that someone via a very effective mail-order campaign, or a book, must have sold these people a bill-of-goods; a formula purporting to reveal the secret of how to watch exacta monitors for profit.

Growing curious, this penster decided to find out how well one could or would do if they based play solely on bet-down horses. The assumption behind this effort was that generally a play-down in the win pool would be reflected in the exacta pool as well. Therefore, any findings relative to win-play bet downs should be equally applicable to exacta bet-downs.

The following shows the procedure used to determine just how well a board watcher would fare if he or she played bet-down horses indiscriminately directly from the tote board or monitors. Note the word indiscriminately. The premise involved was that if educated money existed (as we've previously demonstrated it does) it would usually show up in the last few minutes of play where, due to the volume already in the pool, it would be less apt to attract attention.

Using the program as a convenient means to record betting trends, I used the betting line 10 minutes prior to post time for the initial entry. At this point the public had definitely established its choices and therefore those odds provided a consensus of what the "normal" betting pattern should be.

I again emphasize, as I have elsewhere, that the morning line was totally disregarded.

The 10-minute line was penciled in on the left hand side of my program. From this point on, up to and including the final line, I record every meaningful change. By post time my program appears somewhat as follows (taken from an actual race):

Post Time Chart

Horse	First Line	Second Line	Final Line
1	5	5	5
2	3	5/2	2
3	3	3	7/2
4	7	7	7
5	3/2	8/5	8/5
6	15	15	17

The first line is the 10-minute line. The second one is an intermediate line and the third is the final line. Occasionally I might have had 4 or 5 lines instead of just 3 depending on how the betting trend went.

I performed this record-keeping every time I went to a track for years and saved the programs until I had accumulated data on several thousand races. However, when I started actually making my statistical analysis I used only about 728 races. The trend was so obvious I felt that further research would be redundant and only substantiate what I already could see.

Sames, Lowers and Highers

My approach was to deal only with the first five choices. I felt that going beyond this was a waste of time. I divided each choice into THREE groups: SAME-LOWER-HIGHER.

Same means the horse went off at the same odds as it was at 10 minutes before post. **Lower** means it went off at lower odds than it was 10 minutes before post, and **Higher** means what you think it does, that the horse went off at higher odds than it was 10 minutes before post.

My object was to see where, if any place, a profit was to be made. And whether or not any group fared better than another group. But, mainly I wanted to learn once and for all if this unsophisticated and naive type of board watching could possibly be productive from the player's viewpoint.

So on with the show:

Favorites			
	Same	**Lower**	**Higher**
Races	133	521	74
Won	49=36.8%	181=34.7%	29=39.2%
Bet ($1 Basis)	$133	$521	$74
Return	$124.50	$468.30	$77.80
Loss	$8.50(-6.4%)	$52.70(-10%)	$3.80*
		Profit	5.1%*
Av. Odds	$1.54/1	$1.58/1	$1.68/1

Overall:
259/728 Won (35.5%)
$670.60 Returned from $728.00 Bets = $57.40 lost or -7.8%
Average Odds - $1.00 to $1.59
The only spot that showed a profit in the entire survey.

I use the phrase "unsophisticated and naive" above. The reason I do so is that experience has taught me that one simply cannot afford to be non-selective in racing.

It could be (for example) that a specific group at 5/1 could prove profitable, but all 5/1 shots, played non-selectively cannot possibly be. In the same sense all bet down horses (or all horses going up in the odds) cannot be profitable. In any case these charts prove this to be so.

Second Choice

	Same	Lower	Higher
Races	185	393	148
Won	34=18.3%	73=18.5%	29=15%
Bet	$185 ($1 Basis)	$393.00	$148.00
Return	$123.70	$310.50	$114.80
Loss	$61.30=33.1%	$82.50=21%	$33.20=22%
Av.Odds	$2.63/1	$3.25/1	$2.95/1

Overall:
136/726 Won = 18.7%
$549. Returned from $726.00 Bet = $177.00 lost or 24.4%
Average Odds to $1.00 were $3.03/1

Third Choice

	Same	Lower	Higher
Races	197	281	246
Won	30=15.2%	45=16%	43=17.4%
Bet ($1 Basis)	$197.00	$281.00	$246.00
Return	$154.50	$238.00	$231.00
Loss	$42.50=21.5%	$43.00=15.2%	$15.00/6.1%
Av.Odds	$4.15/1	$4.30/1	$4.37/1

Overall:
118/724 Won = 16.2%
$623.50 Returned from $724.00 Bet = $99.50 lost or 13.3%
Average Odds to $1.00 were $4.28/1

Fourth Choice

	Same	Lower	Higher
Races	180	184	359
Won	22=13%	23=12.4%	35=10%
Bet ($1 Basis)	$180	$184.00	$359.00
Return	$142.00	$156.00	$228.00
Loss	$38.00=21%	$28.00=15%	$131=36.5%
Av.Odds	$5.45/1	$5.78/1	$5.51/1

Overall:

80/723 Won = 11.6%

$526.00 Returned from $723.00 Bet= $197.00 Lost or 27.2%

Average Odds to $1.00 were $6.57/1

Fifth Choice

	Same	Lower	Higher
Races	123	141	459
Won	4=3.2%	6=4.2%	29=6.3%
Bet ($1.00 Basis)	$123	$141.00	$459.00
Return	$31.00	$50.00	$287.00
Loss	$92.00=74%	$91.00=64%	$172=37%
Av.Odds	$6.75/1	$7.33/1	$9/1

Overall:

39/723 Won = 5.3%

$368.00 Returned from $723.00 Bet = $355.00 Lost or 49%

Average Odds to $1.00 were $8.43/1

The reader undoubtedly will note that there are a number of variations in the overall percentage figures from what we normally would expect.

For example, the overall loss for favorites of merely 7.8% is ridiculously low and was brought about because of a higher than normal winning percentage for the period involved. However, such discrepancies are due primarily to the limited number involved in this survey, and undoubtedly would eventually average out.

Nonetheless, our major point relative to bet-downs is quite clear, namely that a profit cannot be made by arbitrarily and indiscriminately playing bet down horses. For example, if one were to play all bet-down favorites indiscriminately (or any other group) it would be a losing proposition.

On the other hand, if we evaluate what happened to all of our **downs** (derived from all five choices) we find the following:

328 out of 1,520 won equalling 21.6%. $3,040.00 was invested on a $2.00 basis, and $2,445.60 was returned. This was a loss of $594.00 equal to 19.5%.

Following the same procedure with the **up** horses we arrive at 12.8% total wins, and a loss equal to 27%. Those remaining at the **same** odds won a greater percentage of races than the **up** horses (17%), but overall losses were also greater, averaging 29.6%.

Now, let's put these figures into table form to make comparisons a bit easier.

	Lower	**Higher**	**Same**
Win Percentage	21.6%	12.8%	17.0%
Overall $ Loss	19.5%	27.0 %	29.6%

We find then, that even though play on all bet downs was not profitable they still showed less of a loss than those from the other two categories. This ties in well with our overall philosophy that in racing less is often more. Or - expressed another way - overlays often prove to be underlays, and vice versa.

Several years after this particular study, we did another one along the same lines involving 1,082 New York races, but this time we concentrated on only the first four choices, and produced the following results.

	Lower	**Higher**	**Same**
Win Percentage	23.5%	16.8%	19.0%
Overall $ Loss	16.0 %	18.8%	23.0%

Obviously, having left the fifth choice out, the percentage of all three groups were improved. The trend however remained the same, and in fact reflects considerable similarity considering that only four choices were used.

Some Conclusions

Several facts from the foregoing stand out and cannot be over-emphasized:

1. It is next to impossible to show a profit from racing by arbitrarily determining to play a particular choice in a particular position. In other words we have seen that there is no choice that will consistently show a profit in any position whatsoever.

2. The trend is for the lower priced, betting choices to afford the player the best break percentage-wise, (Referring to the percentages that one must first compensate for before a profit can be anticipated).

3. If one were to consistently and non-selectively play a "bet down" horse; one would lose much more than his shirt. The same applies to horses that go up in the odds, as well as to those that simply hold their ground and remain the same throughout the betting.

4. We are confronted with the phenomena of there being amazing consistency and predictability relative to the choices in the pari-mutuels and the odds which these choices pay, and the percentage of times they will win.

Possibly this factor was not driven home too strongly in the foregoing due to our concentrating on other matters, but if you wish to know some of these fixed percentages that remain steady year after year (aside from those apparent in our charts, here they are, taken from an analysis of more than 25,000 races throughout the United States at all tracks and under all conditions.

The only variant that one will find (if sufficient races are analyzed) is the minor one brought about by a difference in take and breakage at various tracks.

Racing Constants

Following are, a number of racing's constants which are as certain as death and taxes:

Racing Constants

1. Approximately 5% of all starters go off at odds of $1.00 to $1.95 inclusive.

2. 1% of all starters go off at 95¢ to the dollar or less.

3. Approximately 7.7% of all horses on all tracks every year go off at odds of from 3/1 to 7/2 and of these 21% will win their race season after season.

4. Favorites in 12 horse fields will average 9/5 and win about 27% of all such races.

5. On the other hand favorites in 6 horse fields or less will win 40% of such races and average odds will be 5/4.

These are merely a few unvarying facts. We could go on and on, but the point is made that allowing for certain foreseeable vagaries in the public's betting habits, horses will win directly in ratio to the odds quoted against them and the payoffs will be related to the take and breakage.

A very simple example of this is that all horses with 10% of the pool wagered on them to win will go off at 7/1 and will win 10% of their races returning $80.00 gross (approximately) for each $100.00 bet.

In other words, one could easily and positively predetermine the winning percentage for any specific betting group such as selections at 2/1 or 3/1.

Don't ask me why these facts are true. I don't know. I do know though that through some mathematical natural law they are irrefutable. I did mention the predictable betting vagaries of the public and have already emphasized one such vagary which is the public's tendency to underplay short-priced horses, and to overplay long-priced horses.

Another such tendency is to overplay entries to place. One interesting aspect of the public's wagering habits is that starting with the first race, the ratio of the play in the win pool to that of the play in the show pool might be 3 to 1.

Example: $100,000 bet to win and $33,000 bet to show. By the start of the eighth or ninth race this ration has become anywhere from 10/1 to 14/1.

The story this tells is that the public tends to be ultra-conservative at the start of each racing day. But as the take and breakage exacts its toll, the public tosses its conservative place and show betting out the window and starts ploughing it all in to win in a desperate attempt to recoup that which is simply not re-coupable.

In the last few years many trends which previously prevailed got botched up with the advent of so-called "exotic" wagering. But, on the whole the public still tends to wager more emotionally than logically and the astute player can benefit by this fact.

Let's now concentrate on the favorites and see what we can learn about them.

17. BETTING FAVORITES

Based on many years of observation, it is my belief that the favorite is the key to profitable wagering. Depending on the type favorite involved, a race is either *playable* or not *playable* - the favorite should be bet, or should be bet against.

The favorite is the key as to whether or not a straight bet, exacta or quinella should be played. In other words the favorite should be used to provide the criterion of how best to wager in any particular race.

A vast amount of personal research has revealed that, relative to betting, there are two types of favorites. One I've labelled "Natural," and the other "Created."

Natural and Created Favorites

A **Natural** favorite is one that from the very first betting line is the public's prime choice and remains so right on through to the final line. In some cases two horses will start at similar odds, but eventually one will emerge as the clear-cut choice. In such instances I regard that horse as a **co-Natural** favorite, but treat it the same as a Natural.

It's almost impossible at the conclusion of betting that one of such co-choices will not have a greater amount bet on it, even if the mutuel board indicates they're the same odds. A quick glance at the monies wagered in the win pool will always serve to pinpoint the final favorite. In addition the *Racing Form* will distinguish between two such horses in its result charts.

Here is an actual example taken directly from my track program. The first meaningful money line produced the following odds in this 7-horse field.

Initial Betting Position	Final Line
11/1	17/1
5/1	5/1
4/1	5/1
4/1	6/1
5/2	2/1
10/1	12/1
5/2	2/1

I regarded the two original 5/2 shots as early-line co-favorites. However the eventual winner, who paid $6.20, wound up as the second choice by a margin of only $60. *The Racing Form* result chart showed that both horses went off at $2.10 to $1.00, but indicated the actual favorite by using an asterisk in conjunction with its odds.

Therefore, in this instance the losing 2/1 shot was a Natural favorite. Presumably the $60 that separated these horses at the finish was accounted for via take and breakage.

Opposed to Natural favorites we have the Created favorites. This type is distinguished by NOT having been the early money line favorite. Its status in the betting was attained at some point later on.

An interesting aside to this is that one might tend to view Created favorites as representing the preferences of "insiders," as opposed to Natural favorites that could be deemed the choices of the public-at-large. Consequently, with insiders assumed to be better informed, it would seem that the Createds should prove the superior betting medium. Such, however, is not the case. The Natural favorites appear to hold a marked advantage.

In actuality, I don't think that Natural favorites automatically reflect only the public's choice. My belief is that certain early favorites are made so by unusually large early bets that have little to do with the general public, and that gradually, as more normal betting takes over, these heavily-bet early favorites rise in odds, giving way to the horse that might normally have been the opening-line favorite.

If this hypothesis represents the actual situation, then it follows that this type of early favorite is not created by the public. The question therefore arises as to why big bets would be placed early?

Possibly a betting "syndicate" or a lone bettor making a sizeable wager is sophisticated enough to know that late money attracts more money, and consequently risks lowering the potential payoff.

On the other hand, a horse that is bet early, and in seeming disproportion to the rest of the field, will definitely rise in the odds as betting progresses and thus discourage late betting by the hordes of ubiquitous "board watchers." As money starts coming in on the other horses it can create the illusion that the early favorite is "cold" in the mutuel pool, and possibly result in a larger payoff than that which otherwise might be the case.

But, this is all conjecture. Let's stay with the facts.

Win and Place Results for Created Favorites

About five years ago I analyzed 3,179 consecutive races and found that in 1,038 of them, the favorite was a Created. This implies that approximately 1/3 of all favorites are of this type. From this group of 1,038 races the Createds produced the following results:

> ### Createds Win Rate
> 252 wins/1,038 races = 24.3% (31.6% win rate)
> X $2.00 bet per race
> $2,076.00 **invested** $1,601.00 **return**
> $475.00 **loss** = -22.9% (-16.7%)

If we compare these results to our overall standard for all favorites of 31.6% winners, and a flat bet loss of 16.7%, we readily see that Created favorites offer a speculative opportunity that is somewhat less than top quality.

Expressed differently; they're lousy bets.

What we have on the front end, is a win percentage that is 23% lower than norm (24.3% as against 31.6%), and a dollar percentage loss that's about 37% greater (22.9% as against l6.7%) than our overall average for favorites.

But, maybe Createds fare better on the place end. Let's see.

Createds to Place
458/1038 placed = 44.1% (52.2%)
X $2.00 bet per race
$2,076.00 **invested** $1,707.00 **returned**
$369.00 **loss** = -17.7% (-11.3%)

Nope! The place end doesn't shape up much better.

A place percentage of 44.1% is hardly comparable to our norm of 52.2%. And the percentage of dollar loss, 17.7% as against 11.3%, is not such as to generate much enthusiasm. Note that we've placed the overall percentages, derived from this 3,179 race survey, alongside the current figures to provides a convenient means of comparison.

From the foregoing it can safely be concluded that we don't think highly of Created favorites except in the negative sense. When we pick against favorites we can do so with greater confidence when such favorites are indicated as being Createds.

How much better did Natural favorites do? Let's find out.

Win and Place Results for Natural Favorites

As previously mentioned, the standard used for determining a Natural favorite was that it had to be the opening (or near-opening) money-line top choice. After deducting Created favorites from our total survey of 3,179 consecutive races we were left with 2,151 races that involved Natural favorites. This equalled 67.5% of all, or roughly two out of every three races.

The following tables show how these Natural favorites performed.

Naturals to Win
753 wins/2,141 races = 35.1% (31.6%)
X $2.00 bet per race
$4,282.00 **invested** $3,693.00 **returned**
$589.00 **loss** = -13.7% (-16.7%)

Here's how the place end shapes up.

Naturals to Place

1,203 placed/2,141 races = 56.2% (52.2%)
X $2.00 bet per race
$4,282.00 **invested** $3,934.00 **returned**
$348.00 **loss** = -8.0% (-11.3%)

We've now compared Created favorites to Natural favorites and learned that the Naturals are definitely to be preferred. However, to get an even clearer picture we'll compare these results with the overall results attained when the two categories were combined.

All Favorites to Win and Place

We'll see what would have resulted if theoretically one had bet all 3,179 favorites.

All Favorites to Win

1,005 wins/3,179 races = 31.6% (ALL favorites)
X $2.00 bet per race
$6,358.00 **invested** $5,294.00 **returned**
$ 1,064.00 **loss** = -16.7%

All Favorites to Place

1,661 placed/3,179 races = 52.2%
X $2.00 bet per race
$6,358.00 **invested** $5,641.00 **returned**
$717.00 **loss** = -11.3%

Continuing with our comparison of Createds as against Natural favorites: Createds showed a dollar win loss of 22.9% compared to 16.7% for the 3,179 group as a whole. This 22.9% loss is 6.2%, or 37% greater than our norm of 16.7% (6.2% divided by 16.7% = 37.1%).

Using the same process we'll now check the Naturals against this average and see how they compare. The winning percentage for Natural favorites was 35.1% as against 31.6%. This is an improvement of 3.5% equal to an 11% difference (3.1 is

11% greater than 31.6).

Presenting this in more dramatic terms: Assume that favorites pay an average win mutuel of $5.00. A bettor puts up $2.00 per race and wagers a total of $200.00 on 100 races. If he can get 3-1/2 more winners per 100 races (3.5%) it means he achieves a return on his investment of an additional $17.50 or an 8.5% improvement overall.

How, you might well ask, does the place spot compare to the overall average? We were just about to elaborate.

Created favorites to place produced a loss of 17.7% which is 56% higher than the overall average of 11.3%! The percentage of cashed bets didn't fare too well either; 44.1% as opposed to the overall of 52.2% equals a variant on the minus side of 15.5%.

Natural favorites to place would have enabled their backers to cash 56.2% of their bets compared to only cashing 52.2% if all favorites had been backed. This is an improvement of almost 8%. Dollar-wise, the place end lost only eight cents for every dollar wagered, whereas play on all favorites would have shown 11.3 cents being lost. This represents a 29% improvement in gross return.

There's an interesting sidelight to all of this. The statistics which are reviewed in the foregoing were derived from a study which was done five years prior to our previously reviewed 2,317 race survey. At the time of the first study, computerized and hi-tech handicapping had not as yet attained its current vogue. Note the difference in the overall results as shown in the following table.

	3,179 race survey	**2,317 race survey (5 years later)**
Win %	31.6%	33.6%
Win/Loss	16.7%	18.2%
Place %	52.2%	54.3%
Place/Loss	8.0%	12.3%

In all four instances the latter survey of 2,317 races indicated an improved ability to select winners, but accompanied by greater losses. This is completely in line with our contention that handicappers are currently selecting more winners (we're using favorite results as a criterion), but that these winners are paying less due to the concentration of wagering on "obvious" horses.

High, Low and Average Favorites

Previously we discussed favorites in terms of their being either "Natural" or "Created." We also considered them from the perspective of being "Downs, Ups and Sames." In this section we are going to continue discussing favorites but from the viewpoint of their being either "High," "Low" or "Average." Our objective will be to see if any one of these categories is preferable to the other two from the bettor's point of view.

We should explain that we determined what constituted a High, Low or Average choice by relating the favorite to field size. We were enabled to do this accurately because a number of years back we had been commissioned to devise a slide rule device that would aid a bettor in spotting **board horses** - horses whose odds were out-of-line with anticipated or normal odds.

To create this device we first had to find out what normal odds were. This proved to be a gigantic task involving an analysis of more than 25,000 races.

From this broad perspective, however, we were enabled to determine, along with other data, what the average odds were for favorites relative to each field size; from five betting interests per race on through to 12 per race. This is what we based our conclusions on for the survey now under discussion.

Elsewhere in this text we'll present further details about this 25,000 race survey, but for now let's see what happened within our current trilogy of favorites.

Comparison of Low & Average Favorites with Highs

In an effort to isolate High favorites for the following study, we divided our 2,317 total into two groups. Group one consisted of all Low and Average favorites. Group two was all favorites going off at above average odds (8/5).

We'll revert to our established table format as a means to compare the two groups. Note again that the figures in parenthesis are derived from the basic group of 2,317 races and are intended to afford the reader an easy means of making comparisons.

Low & Average Favorites
408 wins/973 races= 41.9% (33.5%)
X $2.00
$1,946.00 **invested** $1,653.00 **returned** (rounded off to nearest dollar)
$ 293.00 **loss** = -15% (-17.8%)

Low & Average Favorites to Place
616 Placed/973 races = 63.3% (54.6%)
X $2.00
$1,946.00 **invested** $1,799.00 **returned**
$ 147.00 **loss** = -7.6% (-11.7%)

Several factors should be apparent from the above two tables First off, 973 favorites out of a total of 2,317 would indicate that roughly four out of every 10 favorites are either Low or Average. It follows then that 60% (the majority) of all favorites are Highs.

Also, the overall picture is that this select group of Low and Average favorites fared quite a bit better in every way than the larger group of non-selected favorites. It also is obvious that the place end offered an even greater advantage than the win end.

We'll now compare our larger group of Highs with Low and Average favorites.

High Favorites to Win
365 wins/1344 races = 27.2% (33.5%)
x $2.00
$2,688.00 **invested** $2,132.00 **returned**
$556.00 **loss** = -20.7%(-17.8%)

125

High Favorites to Place
642 placed/1,344 races = 47.8% (54.6%)
X $2.00
$2,688.00 **invested** $2,263.00 **returned**
$425.00 **loss** = -15.8%(-11.7%)

There's little need for elaboration. The High favorites are obviously at a marked disadvantage over the Low and Average Favorites, and fare poorly in relationship to our total group of 2,317 favorites.

What would happen if we now deducted Created favorites from our 973 preferred favorites? Well, let's find out.

Keep in mind however that due to the fact that Created favorites tend to be High favorites we won't have too many to account for. In actuality we had 86 with the following results:

Created Low or Average Favorites to Win
32 wins/86 races = 37.2%
X $2.00
$174 **invested** $153.40 **returned**
- $20.60 (-11.8%)

Note that although the Createds won less percentagewise than the L & A group as a whole (37.2 % compared to 41.9%), they showed less of a loss.

The overall group produced a 15% loss whereas the Createds had only an 11.8% deficit. This lesser loss was accounted for by the fact that the Createds' average mutuel prices were greater: $4.77 to $4.05.

It would appear that even when a Created is bet down to the extent of becoming either Low or Average it still remains at a higher level.

Favorites And Exactas

Our interest in the following was to see what would result if we used the favorite as a key horse in Exactas. You will note in our fact sheet (later) that we allow an area for tracking Exacta payoffs comprising any two of our top three choices.

This tracking assumed that a three-horse box was made that included all top three choices in each race. In other words we theoretically played six exactas at a cost of $12.00 per, and regardless of which two of the three ran one-two we cashed. Our six bets would appear as follows:

(F - Favorite, 2 - 2nd choice, 3 - 3rd choice)

F-2	3-F
F-3	2-3
2-F	3-2
6 bets at $2.00 each for a total of $12.00	

We covered 1,834 races in this manner from which 95 races had no Exacta due to fields of five or less entries. This left us with 1,739 races in which we invested $12.00 per race or $20,868.00 total. Let's put this into table form to see the overall results.

Exacta: Three Horse Box

543/1,739 races cashed = 31.2%

X $ 12.00 per race

$20,868.00 **invested** $17,382.00 **returned**

$ 3,486.00 loss = -16.7%

We found that 31.2% of all Exactas involved two of the first three choices, and if one had indiscriminately boxed them in all races, the overall loss would have been 16.7%.

It's of interest to note that this 16.7% is lower than the 17.8% win loss shown for favorites overall.

Our challenge now is to see if this picture can be improved. In an effort to accomplish this we did away with 3-horse boxing, and replaced it with 2-horse boxing using Low and Average favorites as keys boxed with second and third choices as follows:

F - 2	2 - F
F - 3	3 - F
Four Bets at $2.00 each for $8.00 Total	

Utilizing the knowledge gained earlier we decided to save ourselves a bit of work by eliminating High favorites from our investigation. It was obvious that with their relatively poor over-all showing they couldn't possibly improve the exacta picture.

However, if we had used ALL favorites as keys at a cost of $8.00 per race our total investment would have been $8.00 X 1,739 equalling $13,912.00 compared to our previous overall cost of $20,868.00.

Low and Average Favorites as Keys

The following table demonstrates what happens when we used only Low and Average favorites as keys.

Low and Average Favorites Used as Keys
283/801 cashed = 35.3% (31.2%)
X $8.00
$ 6,408.00 **invested** $5,939.00 **returned**
$469.00 **loss** = -7.3% (-16.7%)

The 801 race figure is extracted from a total of 1,658 races and means that L & A favorites were involved in 48% of all races surveyed. This is a somewhat higher average than the 40% indicated earlier.

The seeming discrepancy was brought about because we used fewer races for this survey with the majority of them en-compassing Aqueduct which is notorious for short-field sizes. Short fields tend to have more L & A favorites than larger fields.

Back to our analysis: The figures in parenthesis represent the overall Exacta percentages (using all favorites and six boxes per race) It's pretty obvious that confining play to Low and Average favorites as keys, boxed with second and third choices is a superior approach to simply boxing all three top choices.

Keeping in mind the fact that by reducing the number of our boxes in each race by 33.3% (6 boxes-2 boxes = 33.3% reduc-tion) it would follow that our percentage of cashable chances also should be reduced.

However, in actuality our cashing average was RAISED from 31.2% to 35.3%. This phenomena was due to having eliminated High favorites along with their mediocre win percent of only 27.2% average.

Best of all we reduced our total loss from an average of 16.7% to a much more tolerable one of 7.3%. If we again refer to our earlier discussion, you'll note that this 7.3% is also far less than the 15% loss shown for Low and Average favorites overall.

It's possible at this point that some readers may not grasp the significance of a reduced percentage of loss. For those readers we again wish to emphasize that a major factor insuring that most fans will lose is the 19% tax that operates against the player. And again we make the point that before you can anticipate showing a profit you first have to overcome this formidable roadblock.

Obviously 7.3% (for example) is much easier to overcome than 19%. Skilled and selective handicapping is capable of combatting this relatively low percentage, whereas it is debatable if the same can be said for overcoming 19%.

Look at it this way. There are two racetracks within your access area. Track one takes 20¢ out of every dollar you bet. The other track takes only 7¢ from each dollar. With all other factors being equal, which track would you attend. Of course! You'd go to track two.

We're endeavoring to create a "Track Two" that will give you a much better break than you are now getting from Track One - and make you that much closer to being a winner!

Favorite Exactas and Field Size
(Fields of Eight or Less, Nine or More)

Let's see if we can't improve our Exacta betting to an even greater degree. In an effort to accomplish this we took our 801 preferred races and broke them down into two categories:

1. Fields of eight and less.

2. Fields of nine and over.

We'll consider fields of 8 and less first. The figures in parenthesis will represent the overall percentages given in the foregoing for all L & A favorites. Our table format follows:

Exacta Fields of 8 and Less
179/446 cashed = 40.1% (35.3%)
X $8.00
$3,568.00 **invested** $3,239.00 **returned**
$ 327.00 **loss** (nearest dollar)= -9.2% (-7.3%)

It's apparent that even though we increased our winning percentage it did little good inasmuch as our dollar loss was greater than the 7.3% for the L & A group overall. This underscores the point that winning percentage is meaningless without the price factor being taken into consideration, and visa-versa.

Now let's compare the above results with those derived from fields of nine and more:

Exacta Fields of 9 plus
104/355 = 29.3% (35.3%)
X $8.00
$ 2,840.00 **invested** $2,699.00 **returned**
$ 141.00 **loss** (nearest dollar) =- 5% (-7.3%)

Horrors! Our win percentage is way down particularly in relationship to the 8-horse fields.

But, look what we accomplished as far as dollars and cents are concerned. We reduced the nut in nine horse fields to a mere 5% which should not be too difficult to overcome with a bit of selective handicapping. Just eliminate a couple of those false favorites and you're home free!

Our Exacta research indicates that using L & A favorites as Exacta keys in fields of nine or more horses provides a play in one out of every five races (21%). It also offers the player an advantage dollar-wise over Exactas generally, and a huge advantage over straight win betting on all favorites (5% loss as opposed to a 16.8% loss).

18. LAST-OUT FINISHING POSITIONS

We were curious to see if a relationship existed between a favorite's last-out finishing position and its current winning chance. In order to determine this we did a study of 2,324 races not related to our previously mentioned 2,317 races.

Last-Out Finishing Position and Wins

The survey encompassed 44 weeks of racing and produced 737 winning favorites overall for an average of 31.7%. This was within reasonable range of our anticipated 33%.

We divided the 737 winning favorites into six groups according to how they finished in their previous start, and then followed with the number of wins achieved by each group.

Last-Out Finishing Position	Wins Achieved
FTS (First time starters)	22 (All in maiden races)
lst	171
2nd	133 plus 81 in maiden races
3rd	89 plus 30 in maiden races
4th	53 plus 14 in maiden races
5th and up	114 plus 30 in maiden races

Totals: There were 560 wins in non-maiden races, and 177 maiden wins.

We segregated maiden races to avoid distortions. Without this separation the figures would imply that favorites who finished second in their previous race won a greater percentage of races than last-out winners.

Numerically they did win more, but only because they competed in 177 more races than last-out winners. It should be taken into consideration that 2nd finishers were eligible to compete in all races whereas last-out winning favorites (in fact all previous winners) were excluded from maiden events. This is an important point because maiden races make up about one fourth of all racing.

If we failed to make this distinction it would appear that second finishers earned 29% of the total wins (214/737), and that last-out winners represented only 23% (171/737). All of which is true, but nonetheless sophistic.

The facts are that last-out winners registered 171 of the 560 wins scored in races in which they were eligible to compete. This equals a 30.5% proportion, as opposed to only 133 second horses that scored in this same group of 560; equivalent to only 23.8%. We then see that if we compare like to like the last-out second finishers were at a marked disadvantage when racing against winners.

On the other hand, last-out second favorites excelled in maiden events, registering 81 times out of the total 177 maiden wins. This means that 45.6% of all favored maiden winners had finished second in their previous outing.

This seems to indicate that obvious good physical condition is more important when dealing with maidens then when handicapping races that contain previous winners. With a bit of thought this makes sense, due to the fact that in maiden races, where class has not yet been established, form is much more difficult to conceal whether intentionally or otherwise.

In non-maiden races a horse can enjoy peak racing condition without it being apparent to the casual selector. This is easily accomplished by running the animal a notch or two above its proven class.

A good race in this case might be if the horse in question finished fourth, two lengths off the classier winner. Quite often such a really good race will be overlooked simply because it is not obvious.

Such a situation is far less likely to occur in maiden affairs where it appears that, "What you see is what you get."

The message then that comes across in this survey is that

amongst favorites current physical condition, as suggested by their last-out finishing positions, plays a major role in dictating their chance for success in today's race.

And, one more point worthy of attention: Favorites that were either first or second in their last start represented 52.2% (385/737) of all winning favorites.

Additionally, among maidens, current physical condition would seem to exert an even greater influence, inasmuch as favorites which evinced the greatest degree of fitness (the last-out second finishers) made up almost 46% of the total favorite wins in these events (81/177). This compares to last-out favorite winners with only a 30.5% proportion (171/560) within their own ranks.

Note that we're equating a horse's last-out finishing position with its current condition. This is being done, knowingly, as a matter of convenience. Many factors could mitigate against a last-out finish demonstrating a horse's current racing form. But, overall (recognizing the many exceptions that exist) this is not an unreasonable standard to use.

Examples of possible exceptions:

Horse A ran second last out, but it was six months ago.

Or, Horse B ran second, 12 lengths off the winner on an "off" track, in a 5-horse field. The proper evaluation of such a performance would be difficult.

On the other hand, Horse C, a first time starter, shows a world of early speed, but then falters at the top of the stretch and winds up sixth in a 10-horse field. The chances are that it merely needed that one race as a tightener and is probably dead fit for today's effort.

An Additional 837 Races

Following through on the effort to determine the degree of influence that a horse's last-out finish might exert on its current race, we next checked 837 races covering an 18 week period. We checked to see how many of these races were won by horses that had run first or second in their previous race. Our major interest was to see how well obvious form horses fared, regardless of whether they were favorites or not.

We divided the 837 races into five separate categories that showed the number of races in each group, along with the number and percentage of wins that were scored by horses that were either first or second last out.

Type	Races	Wins Last Out	2nds Last Out
Maiden Claimers	103	None	17 = 16.5% of all
MSW	93	None	20 = 21.5%
Claimers	375	66 = 17.6%	54 = 14.4%
Allowances	199	59 = 29.6%	47 = 23.6%
Stakes & H'caps	67	27 = 40.3%	11 = 16.4%
Totals	837	152 = 23.7%	149 = 17.8%

Some interesting data is evident in the above table. We again see the advantage held by last-out winners over last-out second horses.

Last-out winners were eligible to compete in 641 of the 837 races. They won 152 times equal to 23.7% of all races (keep in mind we are now talking about ALL last-out winners, not just favorites). Many of these races did not have a last-out winner.

Therefore, their overall success rate must be considered as being somewhat above 23.7%. The same, of course, applies to last-out second finishers. Not every race contained a last-out seconders. However, an offsetting factor is that some races contained more than one last out winner, and more than one last out seconder, so on balance we can assume our figures average out.

Wow! Life can sure get complicated.

Our seconders theoretically competed in all 837 races and won 149 times equal to 17.8%. Within the maiden ranks they won a total of 37 times out of 196 races equal to 18.9%.

If we are willing to accept our block of 837 races as being a reasonable representation of all races, it would mean that horses finishing first or second in their previous effort win more than 33% of all races. In the above case the actual numbers were 30l wins out of 837 races equal to 36%.

There's an interesting sidelight to the above table. The maiden claiming races combined with the straight claiming races totalled 478. The last-out first and second horses won 137 of these races equalling 28.7%.

Opposed to this, there were 359 non-claiming races of which our first and second last-out finishers won 164 equal to 45.7%. These figures would certainly lend substance to the theory that better-grade horses are more dependable than the cheaper platers.

High and Low Favorites and Finishing Position

To this point we've established the fact that Low and Average favorites are better investments than High favorites. We next sought to determine what influence, if any, this groups last-out finishing position would have on their performance.

Did last-out winners do best, or didn't it matter? To answer such questions we segregated our L & A favorites into five categories as follows:

> **Five Categories of Favorites**
> 1. Won Last Out
> 2. Second Last Out
> 3. Third Last Out
> 4. Fourth and Worse Last Out
> 5. First Time Starters

One might imagine that the results would be predictable; that the wins would be directly related to last-out finishing positions. We would have thought so too, but it didn't turn out that way.

You may recall we mentioned that in the establishing of a format for our survey of 2,317 races we were obliged to make a number of changes prior to finally creating a set-up that enabled us to record all the information we wanted.

Initially we had not allowed an area wherein we could note last-out finishing positions. The fact that we're using only Natural favorites means that the following is based on 932 L & A choices as opposed to our previous group of 973. This will not exert any meaningful influence on the conclusions, but I thought it best to point out anyway.

L & A Natural Favorites That Won Last-Out (Win & Place)
91 wins/230 races = 39.5% (41.9%)
X $2.00
$460.00 **invested** $342.90 **returned**
$117.00 **loss** (nearest dollar) = -25.4% (-15%)

...To Place
150 placed/230 races= 65.2%(63.3%)
X $2.00
$460.00 **invested** $416.70 **returned**
$43.40 **loss** = -9.4%(-7.6%)

Please note that the figures now in parenthesis are the percentages for the overall Low and Average favorites. They are not the percentage figures for our control group of 2,317 races.

This substitution allows us to conveniently compare how each finishing position within this group compares with the group as a whole. It's apparent from these comparative figures that the last-out winners didn't do well in either the win or place slot.

Average payoff to winners was only $3.77 in contrast to the L & As overall average of $4.05. We mention this because, the high win loss of 25.4% seems to fit in with another of our hypothesis mentioned earlier in this text; namely that one cannot make a profit by going along with the obvious.

And, what can be more obvious than a short-priced horse, that probably was played down, and was a winner last time out? The public goes for this type like a cat goes for catnip, and consequently drives a low-priced favorite down even lower.

L & A Natural Favorites Second Last-Out (Win & Place)
125 wins/303 races = 41.2%(41.9%)
X $2.00
$606.00 **invested** $498.40 **returned**
$108.00 **loss** = -17.8% (-15.0%)

.....To Place

192 placed/303 races= 63.3% (63.3%)
X $2.00
$606.00 **invested** $537.40 **returned**
$68.60 **loss** = -11.3%(-7.6%)

Our second place finishers did better than the last-out winners on the front end but fared slightly worse in the place slot.

L&A Natural Favorites Third Last-Out (Win & Place)

67 wins/161 races = 44.6%(41.9%)
X $2.00
$322.00 **invested** $284.40 **returned**
$37.60 **loss** = -11.7%(-15%)

....To Place

101 placed/161 races = 62.7%(63.3%)
X $2.00
$322.00 **invested** $317.50 **returned**
$4.50 **loss** = -1.4% (-7.6%)

The evidence all seems to be in direct contrast to the results we imagined would be attained; namely that the best previous performance would produce the best result today.

L&A Natural Favorites 4th & Worse Last-Out (Win & Place)

95 wins/203 races = 46.8% (41.9%)
X $2.00
$406.00 **invested** $407.80 **returned**
$1.80 profit compared to a 15% loss overall

...To Place

132 placed/203 races= 65% (63.3%)
X $2.00
$ 406.00 **invested** $400.00 **returned**
$6.00 **loss** = -1.5% (-7.6%)

L & A Natural Favorites First Time Starters
16 wins/35 races = 45.7% (41.9%)
X $2.00
$70.00 **invested** $67.60 **returned**
$2.40 loss =-3.4% (-15%)

...To Place
21 placed/35 races= 60% (63.3%)
X $2.00
$70.00 **invested** $69.40 **returned**
$0.60 broke even (-7.6%)

In reference to First Time Starters, assuming we can draw reasonable conclusions from a mere 35 races, it would seem someone knows something judging by the relatively high win percent compared to all favorites.

It would also appear that the psychology is that FTS will either prove much better or fall short and for this reason they get neglected in the place pool. Because of this apparent thinking the place pool fared well.

However, the more important picture that emerges is that obvious condition seems to generate unwarranted confidence which is reflected in the fact that less obvious favorites do better than the more conspicuous choices. This would seem to apply to the extreme that the less obvious a favorite is, the better bet it becomes.

This thinking would also imply that "horsemen's money" (not "big" money) created most of these low and average favorites who lacked obvious current racing form.

Three Categories of Bettors

You may recall we stated elsewhere that we regarded the mutuel pools as being made up of three distinct categories of bettors:

1. The public which is influenced by newspaper and other handicappers who go strictly by straight data as contained in the *Daily Racing Form.*

2. The horsemen and track personnel; owners, trainers, jockeys, stable help, mutuel clerks, etc. who rely essentially on circulated track information ("inside info").

3. The heavy hitters or big bettors who utilize The Sheets, computer generated information, speed figures, etc.

Our conclusion from all of this is that Low and Average favorites fall into a preferred group, and that one shouldn't let obvious form be the deciding factor when dealing with favorites generally. This, despite the fact that finishing position is a definite plus relative to the winning potential of horses overall.

Horses do tend to win in direct relationship to their last-out finishing positions but, as we have seen, this factor may not be sufficient to compensate for a lowered payoff scale that appears to operate in inverse ratio to last-out performance.

19. SECOND CHOICES

We've discussed favorites and determined that certain types of favorites provide greater profit potential than other types. This being the case it would seem reasonable to conclude that such favorites should not be played against.

Expressed otherwise, those races not having one of our preferred favorites would appear to offer the best opportunity for some other selection to make a good showing. The logical horse to fill this role would be the second choice.

Low-Priced Second Choices Against High Favorites

Putting this hypothesis to the test, and using the knowledge gleaned from checking favorites, we analyzed the results of 1,798 races. From this group we were able to extract 671 races wherein a low-priced second choice ran against a High favorite.

The results derived from this effort are shown below:

L & A Second Choices Against High Favorites
163 wins/671 races = 24.2% (20.9)
X $2.00
$1,342.00 **invested** $1,193.00 **returned**
$149.00 **loss** = -11.1% (-16.02%)

The figures in parenthesis represent the averages achieved by all second choices as indicated in our original master study of 2,317 races. A quick comparison will show that the Low and Average second choices did well when running against High Favorites.

Let's see how they fared on the place end:

> **L & A Second Choices Against Favorites to Place**
> 290 placed/671 races = 43.2% (39.1%)
> X $2.00
> $1,342.00 **invested** $1,198.00 **returned**
> $144.00 **loss** = -10.7% (-15.6%)

Again the second choices did well. In fact they did better to place than to win, and produced almost twice as many cashable bets. This is an important point because nothing is more morale shattering than an extended run of losers. Therefore, anything, or any device, which helps minimize the length of losing streaks, is most desirable.

In this case, for example, what would be the point in betting second choices to win and risking long runs of losers? Remember what we said about favorites? We stated that even though they averaged a win in one race out of every three, they still had been known to lose as many as 30 consecutive races.

In contrast, the above second choices showing a 43% place average are far less apt to have prolonged losing streaks. In addition, the dollar returns are superior to that of the win end.

Note that there were 678 Low and Average second choices against High Favorites in 1,798 races. This means that 37.3% of all races were of this type. It also means that more than one third of all second choices offer good betting prospects.

Overall Second Choices Against All Favorites

As an interesting comparison, in the following we present the overall second-choice figures (against all favorites) derived from these same 1,798 races. You'll note that there is a variation from the average percentages taken from the "master" study of 2,317 races.

The reason why we sometimes are obliged use a lower number of races (rather than the grand total of 2,317) is simply that we conducted our various investigations at different points along the way, as we were in the process of accumulating data.

Example: In the present instance we decided to check second choices at the 1,798 race mark solely because that was all the races we had accumulated at that point.

When we finished, if we felt that sufficient evidence had been compiled (as we did in this case), then we didn't bother to continue investigating further. The chances were that by the time we added enough additional races to be meaningful we had already embarked on another type of investigation and were reluctant to go back if we didn't have sufficient reason for so doing.

All Second Choices to Win
370 wins/1,798 races = 20.5% (24.2%)
X $2.00
$3,596.00 **invested** $2,961.00 **returned**
$635.00 **loss** = -17.6% (-11.1%)

All Second Choices to Place
689 placed/1,798 races = 38.3% (43.2%)
X $2.00
$3,596.00 **invested** $2,997.00 **returned**
$599.00 **loss** = -16.6% (-10.7%)

This time our parenthesized figures represent L & A seconds against High favorites, and indicate that there is considerable difference in both the win and place slots; a difference that definitely favors the L & A second choices.

Looking at our notes we see that this study encompassed the Aqueduct and Belmont meetings, and the results for each track were separately recorded before being combined into the overall group of 1,798 races. We mention this fact because there was a fair-sized variance shown relative to the win-end results between the two tracks. But the place end was extremely stable. Just a point of interest.

Low & Average Second Choices Against All Favorites
We previously related favorites to their last-out finishing position and were somewhat surprised to find that the opposite of what we had anticipated prevailed - that the out-of-money horses

and first-time starters fared much better than the obvious form horses. We concluded from this that many favorites were made such solely on the basis of their obvious good physical condition.

Our further conclusion was that obvious current form alone does not provide sufficient reason to bet a favorite, primarily because they tend to be overbet by the public.

Let's now check out second choices in this regard. The difference between this survey of Low and Average (L & A) second choices, and the previous one of L & A favorites, is that we will evaluate our select group of second choices against all favorites; not simply against High favorites. We used 1,975 races for this survey, and monetary figures, as in most of our examples, will be to the nearest dollar.

L & A 2nd Choice Last-Out Winners (Against all Favorites)
48 wins/240 races = 20% (20.9%)
X $2.00
$480.00 **invested** $341.00 **returned**
$139.00 **loss** = -28.8% (-16.02%)
average price - $7.10 ($8.03)

Parenthesized figures represent the overall average for that particular category using our master group of 2,317 races as the standard. Note that the last-out winners didn't do badly with winning percentages but the dollar and cents return left much to be desired due to the low payoffs involved.

The overall average price of second choices was $8.03. Last out winners though averaged only $7.10. This further substantiates our theory that the public tends to over-estimate and consequently over-bet obvious horses.

L & A Favorite Last-Out Winners to Place
96 placed/240 races = 40% (39.1%)
X $2.00
$480.00 **invested** $366.00 **returned**
$114.20 **loss** = -23.7% (-15.6%)
average price $3.81 ($4.31)

Again second choices took a beating price-wise. The overall average payoff figure is $4.31 but in the above example the average place payoff is only $3.81. However, keep in mind that this is second choices against ALL favorites, inclusive of Low and Average favorites.

L & A 2nd Choice Last-Out Second-Place Finishers to Win

66 wins/288 races = 22.9% (20.9%)

x $2.00

$576.00 **invested** $465.00 **returned**

$111.00 **loss** = -19.2% (-16.02%)

average price $7.04 ($8.03)

L & A 2nd Choice Last-Out Second-Place to Place

123 placed/288 races = 42.7% (39.1%)

X $2.00

$576.00 **invested** $455.00 **returned**

$121.00 **loss** = -21% (-16.02%)

average price $3.70 ($4.31)

Again we note superior performance but lowered mutuels.

L & A 2nd Choices, Last-Out Third-Place Finishers to Win

71 wins/245 races= 28.9% (20.9%)

X $2.00

$490.00 **invested** $538.00 **returned**

$47.00 = 9.7% **profit**

average price $7.56 ($8.03)

We'll save our comment until we complete this survey of last-out finishing positions.

L & A 2nd Choices, Last-Out 3rd Place Finishers to Place

125 placed/245 races = 51% (39.1%)

X $2.00

$ 490.00 **invest** $497.00 **return**

1.4% **profit**

average price $3.97 ($4.31)

L & A 2nd Choices, Last-Out Fourth or Worse to Win
112 wins/490 races = 22.8% (20.9%)
X $2.00
$980.00 **invested** $821.00 **returned**
$159 **loss** = -16.2% (-15.6%)
average price $7.33 ($8.03)

L & A 2nd Choices, Last-Out Fourth or Worse to Place
204 placed/490 races = 41.6% (39.1%)
X $2.00
$980.00 **invested** $827.00 **returned**
$153 **loss** = -15.5% (-15.6%)
average price $4.05 ($4.31)

L & A 2nd Choice FTS
20 wins/67 races = 29.8% (20.9%)
X $2.00
$134.00 **invested** $167.00 **returned**
$33.00 **profit**
average price $8.30 ($8.03)

L & A 2nd Choice FTS to Place
33 placed/ 67 races = 49.2% (39.1%)
X $2.00
$134.00 **invested** $141.00 **returned**
$7.00 **profit**
average price $4.26 ($4.31)

Low and Average Second Choices - Overall Results

Let's see now what the overall results were for the foregoing L&A second choices derived from a total group of 1,975 races.

2nd Choice Overall Results to Win
317 wins/1,330 races= 23.8% (20.9%)
X $2.00
$2660 **invested** $2139 **returned**
$ 531.00 **loss** = -19.9%(-16.02%)

2nd Choice Overall Results to Place
581 placed/1,330 races = 43.69% (39.1%)
X $2.00
$2,660.00 **invest** $2,034.00 **return**
$626 **loss** = -23.5% (-15.6%)

First off, there were 1,330 Low and Average second choices out of 1,975 races. This implies that two out of every three races contain either a Low or Average second choice.

Overall, and disregarding last-out finishing positions, the L & A second choices didn't do well. As might have been expected they won more races but due to poor payoffs in both the win and place slots they showed greater losses than were incurred by second choices generally.

As with Favorites, the major difficulty, as we shall see, was with last-out winners and second-place finishers. Combined they performed as follows:

Favorites, Last-Out Winners and 2nd Place to Win
114 wins/528 races= 21.6% (20.9%)
X $2.00
$1,056 **invested** $806.00 **returned**
$250.00 **loss** = -23.7% (-16.02)
average price $7.07 ($8.03)

Can there be much doubt as to where the problem lies? Combined, these two groups won a greater percentage of races indicating that recent obvious form is certainly an influence on current performance, but again underlying the point that this advantage is too easily seen by the public and the consequence is a decimated payoff.

The place situation follows, in table form:

Favorites, Last-Out Winners & 2nd Place Finishers to Place
219 placed/528 races = 41.5% (39.1)
X $2.00
$1,056.00 **invested** $822.00 **returned**
$234 **loss** = -22.2%(-15.6%)
average price $3.75

Just about everything we said in reference to the win end applies to the place slot.

Conclusion: Similar to other examples we've discussed, non-selective play on Low and Average second choice contenders will do nothing to enhance one's profit potential and will probably increase losses.

Fourth Place and Up Results

Let's now combine our three less obvious finishing positions and see how they fared as a group. We recognize that the fourth-place finishers and up just about held their own but the other two groups evinced a superior performance.

This overall performance synchronizes well with what we discovered relative to the last-out finishing positions of favorites that, overall, the less obvious choices fare best price-wise, and in sufficient degree to offset their generally lower winning percentages.

To Win
203 wins/802 races= 25.3% (20.9%)
X $2.00
$1,604.00 **invested** $1,526.00 **returned**
$78.00 **loss** = -4.9% (-16.02%)
average price $7.51 ($8.03)

To Place
362 placed/802 races= 45% (39.1%)
X $2.00
$1,604.00 **invested** $1,455.00 **return**
$149.00 **loss** = -9.3% (-15.6%)
average price $4.02 ($4.31)

Practically everything we said relative to Low and Average favorites in relationship to last-out finishing position apparently applies equally to Low and Average second choices. Namely, that obvious form will produce more winners, but less obvious form will produce less losses.

Second Choices as Exacta Keys

Along about now you're probably wondering how second choices would fare as Exacta keys. I wondered the same thing and based on the experience with favorites I checked 1,016 races that offered 523 wherein the second choice was Low or Average. You'll see why I stopped at 1,0l6 races.

Again we used four boxes per race at a cost of $8.00 per: 2/1, 2/3, 1,2 and 3/2. This also was based on our experience with favorites.

The results follow in table form:

L & A 2nd Choice as Key Horse in Exacta
147 wins/523 races = 28.1%
X $8.00
$4,184.00 **invested** $3,516.00 **returned**
$668.00 **loss** = -16%

Certainly not particularly encouraging although it compared quite favorably with flat bets to win on second choices. Flat bets cashed only 16.02 times, and showed losses that were almost identical losses (16.02%) to those produced by the Exacta keys.

However, maybe we're being hasty. Let's again do what we did with favorites and break our 523 races up in eight minus, and nine plus field sizes.

The results again follow:

L & A Second Choice as Key in Exacta
Fields of Eight and Less
94 wins/303 races, cashed = 31%
X $8.00
$2,424.00 **invested** $2,030.00 **returned**
$394.00 **loss** = -16.3%

About all that was gained here was that we cashed more bets.

Fields of Nine, Plus
53 wins/220 races, cashed = 24.1%
X $8.00
$1,760.00 **invested** $1486.00 **returned**
$274 **loss** = -15.6%

Conclusion:

No great advantage in using 2nd choices as keys. However, if you choose to do so the L & A second choices in fields of nine and more entries have a slight advantage.

If we eliminated the L & A favorite races from the group of 220 it not only would curtail play considerably but would also lower our percent of cashable bets.

20. COL. STINGO AND ME

After all the numbers we've just waded through, it struck me that the reader might appreciate something in a lighter vein. And I can't think of anything lighter than my initial venture into the racing business. If you've ever wondered how someone becomes a *turf advisor* the following may provide a bit of illumination.

I made a decision in 1946 to go into business. I was 23 and no more of a business man than *Jack the Ripper* was a humanitarian. My commercial awareness was limited to having read that under-capitalization was the major reason new ventures failed. Knowing this, I was confident my savings of $132 would be ample to provide for all contingences.

Being a horse player, it seemed a good idea to combine my vocation with my avocation. I would teach racing fans-by mail-how to select winners. I assumed that most followers of the sport would appreciate such information. The concept was valid, but my qualifications were moot.

My formal education was limited to less than a year of high school. I knew nothing of advertising, copywriting, record kepping or any of the myriad matters about which a business man should be informed. But, none of this deterred me.

The was had ended. The timing seemed right. I rented a small store on a side street in close proximity to the old Jamaica RaceTrack. The rent was $15 per month. After installing a second-hand desk, chair and beat-up typewriter I was in business.

I paid a sign painter to letter *Turf Advisory Service* on the store's one window. The red lettering, backed with a yellow panel, served to shield me and the stark interior of my office from scrutiny by curious neighbors living in this semi-residential area.

Their curiosity aroused, and unable to satisfy it by ordinary means, the local citizenry saw to it that little time elapsed before I was visited by a duo representing themselves as telephone repairmen. As ruses go, this one wasn't particularly clever inasmuch as I didn't have a phone.

Puzzled by the bare interior, my uninvited guests dispensed with subterfuge; flashed their New York City police badges, and demanded to know what I was up to. They inadvertently revealed that their concern was to make certain I wasn't starting a *bookie joint* without having gotten an okay from higher up. I hadn't realized until then the close relationship that existed between God and and the police department.

Cheek burgeoned with tongue, I told them that *Turf Advisory Service* was so named because my business was advising home owners how best to tend their lawns. I could tell my attempt at humor was not appreciated. One of the clues was the way the mean-looking cop took out his blackjack and fondled it.

Recognizing that a legitimate answer might be in order, and stuttering less than usual, I stated, "M-m-my intent is to provide racing enthusiasts with uplifting educational m-m-material designed to enable them to reap greater b-b-benefits from their chosen form of r-r-recreation."

Intially this met with black stares from both, then suddenly the face of the more astute one lit up like an Olympic torch. "Oh," said he, "you mean you're gonna be a tout?" This seemed a bit blunt but I concurred. Concluding nothing illegal was involved my inquisitors shook my hand; wished me luck, and departed.

Having thus been cleared with the neighbors via the police department, I felt my next step should be to do something productive.

Even without a Harvard Business School diploma I realized that to run a mail-order business two things were paramount;

First, I needed something to sell, and secondly I needed someone to whom I could sell. Naively I assumed that to get things moving all I'd have to do would be to devise a racing system; advertise it in an appropriate publication, and wait for the money to pour in.

Part of my assumption was correct. I did a lot of waiting.

The newspaper chosen for my first advertising venture was the now defunct New York Sunday Enquirer which devoted considerable space to horseracing. A flamboyant individual, who employed the pen name "Colonel Stingo," was the racing editor, and wrote a featured column headed, *Yea, Verily.*

The Colonel was a slim, mercurial man of medium height, and about 60 years of age. His white hair was combed back and cascaded down to his collar. He affected a small goatee; a string tie and was the stereotypical image of an antebellum Southern Colonel. In striving to be the sporting world's Walter Winchell, he was prone to inject original, but frequently obtuse phrases into his writings. This tended to make portions of his prose difficult to decipher. But, despite his idiosyncrasies he was a gentleman.

Having lots of gall, but little money to spend for advertising, I sought to enchance the impact of my ad. I arranged an appointment and imposed on the Colonel to give me a favorable review in his column, preferably on the same day my announcement was scheduled to be run. The Colonel's write-up far and away exceeded my expectations. The free blurb was twice the length of my $14 display ad.

I was endeavoring to sell a race-playing system for one dollar. This seemed a modest price for a method of selecting that, as my headline stated, was, guaranteed to produce big winners and huge profits. I was offering the horse player nirvana and all I got in return was 16 orders - even with editorial support. I was discouraged but nonetheless appreciative of the Colonel's kindness and good intentions.

Years later, in the early Fifties, as editor of a nationally distributed racing publication, *American Turf Monthly,* I was provided the opportunity to repay the Colonel by helping him attain celebrity status.

A.J. Liebling was a writer for *The New Yorker* magazine. One day he visited our office seeking a racing personality sufficiently colorful to warrent being featured in his magazine's "Talk of the Town" columns. I regarded my cohorts and myself as a pretty drab bunch and suggested Colonel Stingo as a likely candidate.

Accepting the suggestion, and after interviewing the Colonel, Mr. Liebling apparently agreed with my assessment. The result was a series of three articles titled "Yea, Verily," based on the Colonel's life. They initially appeared in the New Yorker's "Profile" column, but the end product, derived from this series, was a well-received book written by Mr. Liebling titled, *"The Honest Rainmaker."*

It pleased me to think that in some small way I had contributed to its successful publication. A success that was a bit greater than that which my first ad met with.

21. FAVORITES VERSUS FIFTH CHOICES

Being orderly is not one of this race player's most dominant traits. Consequently I go to look up something previously researched, it's akin to seeking the proverbial needle in a haystack.

On the other hand, these invariably fruitless searches often provide opportunities to review material and information that may have been forgotten, overlooked or neglected. In other words, such occasions frequently serve as "refresher courses."

Favorite's Odds, Winning Chances, Field Size

An example occurred recently: While seeking exacta data which had previously (and laboriously) been accumulated, I came across an arithmetic (figural) table which interested me, and almost compensated for my inability to find what I was really looking for. This table showed the relationship between the favorite's odds; its winning chances, and field size. These three factors work in unison, and each exerts an influence on the others.

Example: A favorite held at 2/1 in a field of six horses obviously is not being regarded as highly (by the betting public) as a favorite at similar odds in a field of twelve.

On the other hand, even though the 6-horse-field favorite may be presumed to be of lesser quality than its 12-horse-field cohort, it conceivably could fare better.

Why? Simply because the shorter field presents fewer competitors and less potential problems than would be encountered in the bulkier field. Such, at least, would be the theoretical situation. However, let's see what prevails in actual practice.

The aforementioned table was headed "Favorite," and was segmented into the following five categories:

1. Field Size
2. Win % Expectancy
3. Actual Win %
4. Average Mutuel
5. Gross Return

Number One heading seems self explanatory. **Number Two** pertains to a horse's winning chance relative to field size and regardless of any other condition. This means that in a 5-horse field each horse would have a theoretical 20% winning chance. In a 10-horse field this would be reduced to a 10% chance, etc.

Number Three provides the Actual winning percentage that the favorite averaged in each field size.

Number Four gives the average mutuel payoff, and the fifth heading shows the gross return on a $200 investment (100 wagers at $2 per wager). The following shows the actual table:

Field Size	Win % Expect.	Actual Win %	Aver. Mutuel	Gross Return
5	20	44	$4.20	$185
6	17	39	$4.60	$179
7	14	36	$5.00	$180
8	12.5	34	$5.10	$173
9	11	32	$5.40	$173
10	10	30	$5.70	$171
11	9	29	$5.80	$168
12	8	27	$5.90	$159

You'll note that in the Gross Return column, **Number Five**, there appears to be a discrepancy in that the deterioration of returns is not completely uniform. The "180" is out of sync with the rest of the figures. However, in any valid statistical study there are occasional aberrations which, if pursued long enough, will eventually iron themselves out.

This particular study encompassed several thousand races but apparently was still insufficient for the ironing out process to completely resolve itself.

Fortunately, it doesn't matter. Our prime interest is in observing the overall trend that took place. Note how the favorite's win percentages decreased and its losses increased in direct ratio to field size. Also, what may be surprising to some, is the fact that losses increased as the odds increased. Actually this should offer no surprise inasmuch as the trend conforms with the general scheme of racing.

The definite tendency is for longer odds overall to show greater losses than lesser odds. Expressed otherwise; If one indiscriminately took a group of horses that averaged 7/1 odds and compared it to another group that averaged only 3/1, the chances are great that the 7/1's would show a considerably higher loss than that of the 3/1's.

Of additional interest is the fact that the foregoing table was accompanied by others providing similar data about additional betting choices ranging from the second choice up to and including the fifth choice.

Looking at Fifth Choices

However, we'll discuss only the table for the fifth choice in order to enable us make the most extreme comparison with that of the favorite.

You'll observe in the following that the aberrations previously referred to are even more pronounced with the fifth choice than with the favorite. This is due to the fact that the longer the odds the greater becomes the possibility that extended losing streaks will occur.

It would not be a rarity for a group of horses that averaged 8/1 odds to go 100 or more races without producing a single winner.

As mentioned elsewhere, even relatively short-priced favorites have been known to lose as many as 30 consecutive races. In view of this it would require a huge tabulation of race results to insure that all aberrations with longpriced horses would level out.

Once again, though, it doesn't matter. The long-term trend is still quite evident and goes in the opposite direction to that shown by the favorite; i.e., the greater the odds, and the larger the field, the less loss is incurred.

Note that in the 5-horse field the fifth choice shows a loss of $68 (34%) on a $200 investment (only $132 was returned). Contrarily, the 12-horse field showed a mere $8 loss (4%) with a similar investment.

This too shouldn't be surprising if we keep in mind the simple fact that if the favorite is losing less and winning more frequently, this will have an adverse effect on every other horse in the field. And, of course, the opposite prevails.

Reproduced below is the table that relates to the Fifth choice.

Field Size	Win % Expect.	Actual Win %	Aver. Mutuel	Gross Return
5	20	4.75	$27.70	$132
6	17	7.25	21.00	152
7	14	8.25	21.10	174
8	12.5	8.00	19.10	153
9	11	8.00	19.40	155
10	10	7.75	20.40	158
11	9	6.75	17.20	116
12	8	8.75	22.00	192

Favorite as the Key Element

The information to be gleaned from the foregoing is simply to keep in mind that the favorite provides the key to practically every race. Those races with short-priced favorites are to be approached with caution if one is considering a bet on other than the chalk. The other side of the coin is that the longer the price on the favorite and the larger the field size the greater becomes one's chance to come up with a good priced winner.

22. FRONT RUNNER, WITH PACE, OFF PACE

We had long felt that early speed horses did best at short distances and that the trend was for off-pace or strong-finishing horses to dominate at the longer distances. However, we've observed that quite often opinion and fact do not coincide. On this basis we decided to do a little research.

1,528 Race Survey

We conducted an analysis of 1,528 races that showed conclusively that front runners dominate the winner's circle in sprints, and off-pace horses come into their own as distance lengthens.

The interesting aspect of this survey was that the trend prevailed in exact ratio to the distance involved. That is to say that Front Runners (FR) were No.1 at six furlongs, but were reduced to a No.3 status at 1-1/8 miles.

The opposite also prevailed. Off-pace horses were rated No.3 in sprints, and became No.1 in routes of 1-1/16 and more miles. A third category, with-pace horses (WP), were ranked either No.1 or No. 2 for all distances. The conclusion being that the WPs were best or safest for play on an all-around basis.

Our criteria for the three categories were:

1. FR were those horses that in their last effort had either set the pace up to the stretch run or never been worse than one length off the leader.

2. WP implied horses that had never been further back than three lengths off leader in last effort.

3. The OP group included all horses that made up more than three full lengths in the stretch run. The actual results follow:

	6-furlongs	7-furlongs	Mile	1-1/16	1-1/8
FR	323/747	82/260	32/136	43/187	51/198
	42%	31%	23%	23%	21%
WP	282/747	101/260	63/136	79/187	72/198
	38%	39%	46%	42%	36%
OP	142/747	77/260	41/136	65/187	75/198

FR - Front Runner   WP - With Pace   OP - Off Pace

Note how the winning percentage of the front runners almost consistently declines as the distance is stretched out, and contrarily, how the off-pace horses steadily improve with each lengthened bit of real estate. Also observe the reliability of the with-pace runners.

Speed Handicapping

We also would like to call attention to the fact that almost 50% of all races checked were at 6-furlongs (747 against 781). Mention is made of this due to the fact that I've long suspected that the best and truest approach for speed advocates would be to use 6-furlong races *only* for their speed handicapping.

You may have noticed that I make little mention of speed or pace as a useful handicapping aid. This is no oversight.

Your scribe believes that speed handicapping is not the best approach to winners. However, with almost half of all races being held at the popular 6-furlong distance, it would certainly seem that speed comparisons would work best and have greater validity if confined to this distance.

My impression is that speed handicappers make an error similar to that which is common to many selectors. They latch on to one isolated approach and endeavor to make it cover all circumstances. It seems logical that fast times would be a meaningful factor at abbreviated distances, but when it comes to routes other handicapping considerations assume greater importance and cloud the picture considerably; endurance, weight, class, jockey skill, ability to be rated, etc.

Speed Ratings and Track Variant System

A number of years back I marketed a system that had a very simple premise. It was based on combining the older Daily Racing Form speed ratings and track variants.

Example: Speed rating, 84 PLUS track variant of 10 equals final rating of ninety four. The horse that had the highest last out overall rating was the selection with only certain sensible qualifiers such as:

I. Must have run within 30 days.
2. Must have have run over same track.
3. Must not be picking up excessive weight.
4. Track condition must be similar to that of previous outing.

That was just about it. Surprisingly this overly simplified approach did remarkably well, and showed a substantial winning percentage, as well as equally substantial flat-bet profits.

Early Speed vs. Off-Pace Horses

But, the important feature was that the workout of more than 500 consecutive races, that accompanied the system's rules, was confined to 6-furlong contests only.

Relative to the foregoing examination of front runners, etc, we did another study that concentrated on **FR** (early speed horses), as against **OP** horses (strong finishers). This involved 1,253 races and showed that 462 winners or 37% were of the two types surveyed. In this instance our standard for strong finishers was that they had to show a gain of more than four lengths from start to finish in last effort.

The conclusions tended to support the findings of our previous survey inasmuch as they implied that the huge majority of winners (63%) at all distances were **WP** (with pace) horses.

Last-Out Finishes

The following offers the actual breakdown of performance by front runners, early-speed horses that either set pace or remained within one length of the front runner (**ES** - Early Speed).

ES	LAST-OUT
81	Won
68	Second
48	Third
83	4th or worse
276 Total	

By way of comparison the following indicates how OP (Off-Pace) horses fared.

OP	LAST-OUT
72	Won
40	Second
21	Third
53	4th or worse
186 Total	

The foregoing figures would indicate that the early-speed horses enjoy a marked advantage over strong finishers with a ratio of 59% for ES as against 41% for OP.

In both examples the last-out winners would appear to have a strong edge. It would also be obvious that an animal's chance of success is directly related to its last-out finish position. Note how this is invariable.

The category of "4th or worse" is not a contradiction inasmuch as this group includes ALL horses that finished worse than third in their last race. This is roughly six times the number of horses from any one of the first three groups.

Sprints, Mile Races, Routes

The following provides a breakdown of distance performance for the two groups.

SPRINTS
ES 177 (72%)
OP 68 (28%)

MILE RACES
ES 19 (58%)
OP 14 (42%)

161

ROUTES
ES 80　(43.5%)
OP 104　(56.5%)

It's of interest to note how the trend is to modify the advantage of the early-speed horses as distance lengthens. This is in full accord with our first survey referred to at the beginning of this chapter.

23. ARE STABLE ENTRIES GOOD BETS?

There is a tendency on the part of many players to bet entries feeling that two or more for the price of one must be a bargain. This concept can prove costly.

Our research has uncovered two seemingly contradictory facts. *1. Favored entries (certain ones - not all) are bargains; 2. Entries other than favorites are not.*

All too often, half of a 2-horse entry may loom as a genuine contender whereas the other is a near-impossibility. If the true contender was running alone it might be 7/2 but due to the fact it's part of an entry, the public exaggerates its chance and the entry goes off at 5/2 or less even though one half of the entry stands no chance whatever.

Invariably, stable entries are bet out of proportion to their winning chances, and for this reason alone entries are rarely good bets.

Natural and Created Favorites

You cannot consistently take the short end of the odds and expect to come out a winner over any extended period of time. This does not seem to apply to those favorite entires that we would term "natural" favorites as opposed to created favorites.

A **natural favorite** is one that is the opening *money-line* favorite (which is not necessarily the same as the morning-line favorite), and winds up as the post-time (final line) favorite.

A **created favorite** is one that was not the opening money-line favorite but does wind up as the post-time favorite.

We checked 346 natural favorite stable-entries covering a period of 28 months of New York racing. They won 142 of their races (41%) and placed 226 times (65%). This compares to a norm for all favorites of approximately 32% and 53%.

Favorites overall show at 16% win loss and a 12% place loss. Our group of favored entries did considerably better. A $2.00 flat bet to win would have required an investment of $692.00 with the return being $675.20; equal to a win loss of only 2% overall. Far better than the norm of 16%.

On the place end, the return on a similar investment was $703.00 equal to a profit of $11.00 (1% plus). The profit can probably be chalked up to the fact that on occasion an entry will run 1-2 and create a considerable overlay frequently paying more to place than to win.

So we see that selective betting on favored entries can produce bargains. Now let's examine the situation with entries overall.

Overall Stable Entries

Keep in mind that if a trainer has two "live" ones he'd be foolish under ordinary circumstances not to run them in separate races. Why take a beating on price, and risk losing out on a second win purse unnecessarily? Horses are too fragile for a trainer to figure, "Well, if I only get place money here, I can still win next time." Next time may never come.

True, there are circumstances wherein both halves of an entry may be well meant, but such instances are rare. Example: On occasion the horses involved may be trained by two different individuals. However, due to overlapping interests they are obliged to race as a single betting unit.

In such cases it's reasonable to assume both could be trying to win. There are other situations as well, such as in major stake races, but as a rule of thumb, you can assume that only one horse is live, and even then it's questionable why the trainer chose to run it as an entry.

Regardless, we started with the intent to check all entries but before long realized it was a waste of time. It quickly became apparent that continuing the check would be futile. Entries, per se were obviously not a profitable or advisable investment. Therefore, we adopted a totally different approach.

Stable Entries and Top Trainers

We concluded that if indiscriminate play on all entries was a financial disaster (as it obviously was) it was possible that only those entered by the more talented trainers might show a profit possibility.

With this as a premise, and having access to records covering more than six full years of the training activities of Phil Johnson, Dick Dutrow and John Lenzini, Jr, we decided to see how these individuals, who represent the top echelon of New York trainers, fared with their stable entries.

If they couldn't produce an overall profit for us than we had to conclude no one could.

Our approach was pretty straight forward. We first determined what was normal for this trio, percentage-wise and dollar-wise. Then we compared the performance of their entries with this established norm.

Let's begin by presenting what the normal combined averages were for these three trainers. During the period covered, they started - as a group - 8010 times, and won 1,387 times achieving an exceptionally high 17% average.

If a trainer enters more than 100 horses within any one year and wins 15% of his races he is performing above average.

Keep in mind that the greater the volume, the more difficult it becomes to maintain a high average. These three horsemen flooded the track programs with volume and still managed to maintain a tremendously high winning standard.

But - how did they fare in the payoff department? Recognizing that the track "take and breakage" approximates 19%, we must then consider this as the normal or average loss. In other words any approach that loses less than 19% must be regarded as being better than normal; a loss greater than 19% is then obviously, worse than normal.

Our figures indicate that if one played all horses entered by this trio on a $2.00 flat bet basis, $16,020 would have been required. This produced a loss of $2,697 equal to 16%. We grant that this is nothing to grow ecstatic about, but keep in mind this was indiscriminate play and still managed a front-end loss below normal and on a par with the low loss favorites produced.

On the whole it was a good showing and indicates one could do worse than to confine selective play to the top trainers.

Okay, we now see that the results these trainers produced were better than average. We therefore have every right to think that their stable entries too might produce results above average - show at least a 17% win average and a loss below 19%.

In actuality they ran 1085 entries that produced only 143 winners. This was an average of 13% or 23% **below** their normal winning average. Doesn't seem as if there's much profit possibility here, but let's find out. Maybe the entries had better payoffs to compensate for their low winning average.

Not so! Overall returns were a disaster. The loss was just short of 25%. It's safe to assume that if the entries handled by these trainers didn't produce encouraging results then rest assured, run-of-the mill trainers will not do better.

Conclusion:

The only play worth considering appears to be entries that conform to our natural favorite category. The best spot is the place end. All entries should be considered carefully before betting. Entries win, but not often enough at proper odds to be classified as "good bets." Be cautious.

24. HOW TO CREATE YOUR OWN PRICE LINE

Most seasoned players have a pretty good concept of which horses in a given race should either be vying for favoritism, or be the first and second choices. It is doubtful, however, if most players have the knowledge to go much beyond this point. The chances are that they would be hard put to state what the *actual* odds should be on the the first two choices, and probably would be totally at sea if requested to make a price line for every horse in a race.

This is understandable because in the viewpoint of the average fan he has no need to create his own line. He has the morning line as given in the track's program, and in addition he has the betting line once the money starts coming in to the mutuels. Who needs to make their own line when it's already made? The answer is, YOU do.

The Importance of the Natural Line

You need to take the trouble to create your own price line because you cannot rely on the accuracy of a track's morning line, or on the accuracy of the general public's early-money lines. To be a winner, you need to know when meaningful variations from the norm occur.

We'll refer to our creation of a line as being a **Natural Line** and will use it as our gauge for judging when horses appear "cold" or are receiving heavier than expected mutuel play. But, before explaining how to create a Natural line let's see if we can first understand what betting factions influence the odds.

Our assumption will be that three major betting factions exist. We'll look closely at all three betting interests shortly. Our reason for so doing is that if we understand the betting components underlying each race we will be in a better position to interpret whatever wagering trend is taking place.

The rationale behind creating one's own comparative (Natural) line is the recognition that racing is a game of dollars and cents. Money literally is what make the mare go 'round.

Consequently, a serious-minded player would be well advised to make every effort to determine in each race which horses are being bet and which are not. More specifically, he should determine which horses are being UNDERBET and which horses are being OVERBET. And - by which betting group?

And, as we've indicated elsewhere in this text, generally speaking the assumption should be that more is less, and less is more.

This means that the so-called overlays should be looked on with suspicion, and that the underlays should be given careful consideration in order to determine if there might not be good reason for the heavy play they attracted.

This does not imply that a player should blindly go with the flow. But what it does mean is that he should learn to subjugate his ego and heed the warning signs. This business of subjugating one's ego is not something to be glossed over. It's a very important part of successful handicapping and, along with impulsive betting, is probably one of the toughest psychological factors that one must learn to control.

To a great degree handicapping is an exercise in ego in which we seek to demonstrate our knowledge, astuteness and skill. Therefore when a betting trend appears to be in opposition to our opinion it is difficult to concede that maybe, just maybe, we might be wrong and should re-examine our analysis. The tendency is to ignore the warning signs.

We are not suggesting that one should be namby pamby and swayed by every betting breeze that blows. Of course not, but one should be open-minded enough to heed what the odds-board might be trying to tell you. After listening to its "argument," which may oppose your original thinking, then and only then decide if you either should stay with your original choice, or reassess the situation.

The ability to create your own Natural (odds) line will provide you with a formidable weapon for your handicapping arsenal. It will put you in the enviable position of being able to objectively assess mutuel play and then - based on evidence and not mere opinion - come up with a sounder decision than might otherwise have been the case.

There are many handicappers who will have little need to physically perform the drudgery of creating a Natural line due to the fact that through years of observation they have learned to judge, frequently by instinct, when a horse is out of line.

For example, as I write this, Chris Antley is red hot. He's the leading rider and the public is aware that he's a hustling jock who gives his best every time. In consequence his mounts frequently get over bet.

Now, let's assume a hypothetical race wherein the morning-line maker has Antley's mount listed as a second choice at 5/2, in a 7-horse field, and we'll further assume that the anticipated favorite is listed at 9/5. Next, we'll assume that the morning-line choice remains at 9/5 near post, and Antley's mount either stays at 5/2 or worse, goes up to 3/1.

Any player whose instincts have been honed by having watched thousands of races would realize that for all practical purposes Antley's mount has little need to be refrigerated. It's already ice cold. Also, we might add, the favorite is not exactly red hot either. In a case such as this an alert punter would be well advised to look beyond these first two choices for a potential winner.

Okay this is well and good for the seasoned, observant fan. It is also well and good when situations arise that are as obvious as the one we described. But, how does the less-sophisticated fan spot out-of-line horses, and how does anyone spot the more subtle betting variations that take place? The answer to both questions is create your own Natural line.

To create a line in the way that we'll advise requires a bit of effort. It can take up to 10 minutes for each race in order to put a Natural line together. To some this may sound too demanding and tedious. We can understand that, and if this applies to you we advise that this chapter should simply be skipped. Line making is evidently not your forte. For those others, however, who understand that the ability to create a valid betting line can be important, we offer the following.

THE THREE BETTING GROUPS

It's your scribe's belief that betting patterns are influenced by three fundamental groups. The first two are pretty widely recognized. It's the third group that tends to be overlooked. Each group has a message to convey and the bettor should heed it.

I. The Public-at-Large

The first and most obvious group represents the public-at-large. Its selections are based primarily on the opinions of public (newspaper) selectors.

These public handicapper-selectors in turn have based their conclusions essentially on information derived from the *Daily Racing Form* and, as a group, have followed the same procedure as that which was followed by private selectors. Therefore, the public selectors do no more than reflect the opinions of private handicappers inasmuch as they both, so to speak, are drinking from the same well.

One can also lump the track's morning-line maker in with private handicappers as an additional source of public influence.

The only difference between the overall opinions of public and private handicappers then is that the private handicappers have an edge due to the fact they have access to last-minute information not available to newspaper handicappers. Therefore, briefly stated, the public's betting activity reflects the opinions of orthodox handicappers generally.

The result of this combined public opinion is seen in the early betting patterns. In other words the early odds usually indicate the choices made by the general public at both the track and at OTB. However, there is a caveat to this which we will detail shortly.

2. The Big-Money Bettors

The second group which influences parimutuel betting patterns has been discussed in detail elsewhere in this tome. We refer to the "big money" bettors, and the point has been made that they have access to data which is in excess of that which is available to the public-at-large; computerized speed figures, data-bank trainer information, etc. The money from this group can readily be identified because it invariably comes in very late in the betting.

3. The Race-Trackers

The third group that wields an influence on the odds is comprised of race-trackers, and its influence is not as widely recognized as that of the first two. The term **race-tracker** in this context is intended as a coverall for those people employed at the track inclusive of the shedrow populace, mutuel department personnel, office personnel, and horsemen generally.

It is unusual (but not unknown) to find anyone within this segment to be a substantial bettor. Individual bets tend to run the gamut from $2.00 on up to $50.00, but, when these small bets are combined, the gross is substantial. The betting opinion expressed by this group, unlike the opinions of the other two groups, are NOT based on documented detail derived from recorded sources such as the Daily Racing Form or data banks.

Primarily the race-trackers arrive at their conclusions on the basis of first-hand observation of the horses themselves. Those bettors who fall within this category, but whose opinions are not based on first-hand observation, arrive at their conclusions via rumor.

That is to say that word travels fast around a racetrack. Maybe a rumor circulates that Horse A has a bleeding problem, or Horse B had a fast work not caught by the clockers, or Horse C walked its stall all night and is off feed, etc.

The betting which originates with track personnel tends, like that of the public-at-large, to be bet early.

This fact gives rise to the question, "How then does one differentiate it from the public's early-money betting?"

The answer is that quite often "stable" money is non-conformist money. Expressed otherwise, this is the type of action that can make an early-money line favorite out of a horse that wasn't picked one, two or three by most newspaper selectors.

Such unanticipated betting represents the positive aspect of "inside information."

On the other hand, money from this source can also change a potentially red hot 6/5 morning-line favorite into an ice cold 5/2 favorite simply by not adding its support. This is a reflection of the negative aspect of the same inside information. In other words its action was held back from one horse and probably sought greener pastures elsewhere within the mutuel pool.

The reason why one should be aware of these various large betting cliques is because each one is trying to tell the bettor something. In the first example the statement being made is that an *objective* analysis indicates that the race shapes up legitimately in accord with the early, anticipated odds.

The second group states, in effect, "According to our ***additional*** knowledge the early odds should be modified to reflect our opinion."

Then the final group is saying to the other two, "Look, you guys are pretty good with your logical conclusions based on past history but we deal with these horses physically, and on the basis of our *subjective* knowledge, you're away off base." Regardless, these three messages should be looked for and heeded. The best way to insure that the messages of the mutuels will be understood is to have a comparative (Natural) line to use as your gauge.

How to Create a Natural Line

I have given this matter of creating a reliable line considerable thought and have subjected it to a vast amount of trial-and-error experimentation. The end result has been that our Natural line is a valid one but the creating of it is somewhat more cumbersome than we would have liked.

The making of a Natural line requires that one have access to the selections of eleven newspaper selectors. In my case I use the six from the Daily Racing Form, and the five that are given in the New York Daily News. If you have access to the opinions of only 10 selectors you could use the track's morning line as the eleventh.

Each selection by each of the 11 handicappers receives a rating that ranges from one to three. Therefore the absolute top rating that a horse could earn would be 33 points and this would be in the unlikely circumstance that all 11 selectors (do not use consensus choices) latched onto the same horse.

Note that we ignore "Best Bets."

Each selector's first choice is rated at three points. A second choice is given two points and a third choice is assigned one point.

Now, these values may seem arbitrary, but the fact is they were arrived at after considerable thought. In effect a second choice is being assigned 66% of the value of a first choice, and a third choice is being accorded a 33% winning chance compared to that of the first choice and — only half the chance of winning that is accorded to a second choice.

How to Convert Points into Equivalent Odds

At this juncture we ran into major problems. When we started out the thought was that we'd simply convert our points into odds. There were 66 total points which equalled 100%, and superficially it seemed that if we first converted our points into percentages then it would be a simple matter to convert the percentages into equivalent odds. For example, Horse A earns 22 points which equals 33.3% of sixty- six. Not allowing for "take and breakage" this would then convert to 2/1 odds.

However, seeing as take and breakage does exist we would then have to assume a mutuel pool of approximately 82% rather than the 100% which would prevail in that never, never land of no taxes.

Therefore, recognizing that we'd have only an 82% total to

pay out, the prospective odds on Horse A would be reduced to approximately 8/5. This figure was arrived at by reducing our original 2/1 odds by 18% which left 1.64/1 or approximately 8/5 as the final odds.

This was the procedure which was originally followed. But, after having checked thousands of these assigned odds, and after comparing them to the actual post time odds the conclusion arrived at was that they were not accurate enough. This inaccuracy could have been the result of many potential qualifiers including the betting quirks of the public itself. We refer to such foibles as over-betting stable entries, favoring certain trainers and jockeys, etc. But, primarily the discrepancies were due to the fact that a number of horses in each race received no numerical rating. This alone would tend to upset any forecast of what the final odds should be.

In order to adjust and correct our initial ratings (odds) we did the following. We created columns on a sheet of paper with headings that ranged from 3/5 (a horse that earned 33 points) on up to 40/1 (a horse that earned only one point). Then beneath these headings, which represented our original assigned odds, we recorded from each day's racing charts what the actual odds were for each of the "rated" horses in each race.

For example:

Our Initial Odds:	2/1	5/2	3/1	7/2
	9/5	7/2	3/1	4/1
	5/2	3/1	5/2	7/2
	8/5	5/2	4/1	5/2

This record keeping was continued for many hundreds of races and represented a recording of multi-thousands of final odds. When a sufficient number had been accumulated the next task was to average all figures under each heading in order to arrive at a final conclusion as to what final odds our point system represented on average.

Assume that under the 2/1 heading we recorded 900 final points that averaged out to 8/5 rather than our initial 2/1 odds. With this as our basis we then concluded that all initial 2/1 equivalent odds selections should automatically get converted to 8/5 inasmuch as our primary figure was too generous. We followed this procedure for every odds-group.

Cheer up! You really don't have to know how we arrived at our conclusions but we felt that an explanation would give you more confidence in the approach. Just remember that points are established for each horse by using all three selections of each of 11 public handicappers. Each selection is scored as follows:

> 1st Choice is 3 points
> 2nd Choice is 2 points
> 3rd Choice is 1 point

We now use the table below to convert points into meaningful odds:

Points	Equivalent Odds	Points	Equivalent Odds
1	15/1	17,18,19	3/1
2	12/1	20,21	5/2
3	10/1	22,23	2/1
4	9/1	24	9/5
5	8/1	25,26	8/5
6,7	7/1	27,28	3/2
8,9	6/1	29	7/5
10	5/1	30,31	6/5
11,12	9/2	33	1/1 and less
13,14	4/1		
15,16	7/2		

The Concept Further Explained

Just to insure that the concept is understood: The conversion of points into Natural (equivalent) odds is not directly related to any arithmetics. The final odds which we arrive at are more akin to the relationship which was established by checking and re-checking our initial set of odds against thousands of race charts that showed the actual closing prices of all horses involved.

The initial odds were then corrected according to how each set of closing odds averaged out.

As a consequence, our Natural or Equivalent odds now incorporate not only the mathematical element but the idiosyncrasies of the human element as well. It's only by recognizing the many "normal abnormalities" that we can hope to pinpoint whatever genuine deviant tendencies that might occur.

Sound confusing? Not really.

If we recognize that the public (as an example) will tend to overbet stable entries then we also won't think it out of line when an entry that should be 2/1 goes off at 8/5 - we would recognize that this is a normal mutuel aberration.

Using the Natural Line

Okay! We now know how to make a Natural line. What do we do with it?

First let me explain the way that I go about the mechanics of figuring the Natural or Equivalent line. The first thing I do is cut out the selector's box from the daily paper. I use scotch tape to attach it conveniently below the selector's box in the *Daily Racing Form*. In this way I've got my 11 handicappers conveniently together.

I next take out a small looseleaf pocket notebook which I carry and which contains my conversion table. Using a blank page from the notebook I figure out what the Natural odds should be and when I finish I transfer the results to the left side of my program with the odds for each horse being properly placed alongside the horse's name and program number.

My next step is to wait until there is about from $20,000 to $30,000 in the win pool (enough to be regarded as a meaningful amount). I then enter this "money line" to the right of my Natural line. Note that the track's morning line is completely ignored.

At this point my program might appear somewhat as follows in a 7-horse field:

Horse	Natural Odds	Public's Money Line
1	6/1	5/1
2	9/2	5/1
3	10/1	8/1
4	0	9/2
5	8/5	2/1
6	8/1	8/1
7	4/1	7/2

Note also that the No.4 horse did not receive a Natural line rating, meaning that it was not mentioned by any one of our 11 selectors but for some reason was getting relatively heavy play. However, it is not as yet considered a bet.

Now comes the kicker. So far we have established what the Public's money line is, and what our Natural line is. What we will look for from this point on is to see if any horse goes to post BELOW both of these established lines. Example: If Horse No. 5 went off at 9/5 it would not be a play, simply because its final odds are not below BOTH established lines.

Number 4, on the other hand, could be a play if it went off at 4/1 or less inasmuch as 4/1 would be below 9/2 and certainly below the zero we assigned it.

Note we indicate that a horse or certain horses could be a play if they fall below our two established lines, but this does not mean it or they necessarily will be a play. However, the opposite definitely prevails; if they go off at the same or higher odds they CANNOT be played.

When Does a Bet-Down Actually Become a Play?

Ideally this line-making approach should be regarded as an adjunct to one's own handicapping to the extent that it would be used to either confirm or question the correctness of one's handicapping.

In other words it makes an ideal control and relates to our previous discussion about not letting ego lead to myopia. Select your contender and then use the two established lines to confirm the rightness of your selection. If you do not get confirmation you should then reconsider your choice.

This, as we say, is the ideal approach but many readers will want something more definite.

Therefore, we offer the following.

In exploring this method we checked 5,200 races, and a number of different approaches in an effort to determine what worked best. Almost needless to emphasize, nothing worked better than employing one's own good judgement.

However, on a strictly mechanical basis, we determined that those races with *single* bet downs, were superior prospects to those which had multiple bet downs. A little more than half of our 5,200 were of this type (having only one bet down).

From this group we had 40% winners that showed a 15% flat bet profit, and on the place end we scored with 60% of our selections and produced a 14% profit. Obviously there's no guarantee that these figures will always prevail but they certainly attest to the overall merit of the approach.

My suggestion would be to concentrate on the place end due to the fact that the potential profit is about the same as that of the win end, but the success rate achieved of 60% is considerably higher. We feel that this is important because it precludes the likelihood of running into extended losing streaks. And, as mentioned elsewhere, long losing streaks do very little to bolster one's morale.

The creating of one's own price line is a somewhat laborious procedure but our experience indicates that the effort that goes into it is worthwhile, and is a key step in making one a winner!

25. HOW TO MAINTAIN RECORDS

Success in most financial ventures requires full knowledge of what is happening. And in race-track betting, as in business, there's only one way to insure having this knowledge; **you must keep detailed records!**

Why? There are many reasons but foremost among them is the fact that this is the only approach that will enable you to recognize your strengths and weaknesses. Detailed, conscientious record-keeping not only will improve your win-ability, but it is absolutely essential if profitable handicapping is your goal.

This, of course, assumes that such records will periodically be reviewed and analyzed by to determine the debits and credits of whatever handicapping approach is being used. It also assumes that you will be sensible enough to take advantage of whatever is learned, and will not compulsively continue pursuing what may turn out to be a completely wrong approach.

The Importance of Keeping Good Records

Periodic analyzing is, in part, what a businessman pays a good accountant to do, and the racing fan who keeps records should do no less when acting as his own accountant. To a degree, the longer one's detailed accounting is extended, the greater will be the knowledge that can be gleaned. For this reason it is necessary to persist even when the temptation is strong to say, "The hell with it."

It's unfortunate that many, if not most, race players seem to suffer from a common ailment and approach the game from one direction; one they've grown comfortable with, and they appear unable, or unwilling to change. This stick-to-itness is admirable if what one is doing is producing profits. If, however, you're one of those not so fortunate, it will pay to heed this chapter's suggestions. The concepts offered can be of immeasurable help to any raceplayer.

We've mentioned it before, but it is worth repeating; racing is highly competitive. You are not playing against the racetrack. You are bucking heads with your fellow fan. Any profits that may be forthcoming must find their way from his pockets into yours. There's no other way.

Therefore, it follows that your **only** chance to win will be if are willing to study more and get to really know more; unlike some players who, despite being chronic losers, *think* they know more. It also follows that you must be willing to make a greater and more intelligent effort.

Applying a businessman's approach to handicapping will put you on the right track, and there's no gag intended. The fact is that a properly maintained, "bookkeeping" system not only will improve one's handicapping, but will also pinpoint the virtues and vices relative to one's betting habits.

We see therefore that successful horseplaying demands that a two-pronged approach be employed. Handicapping ability is one part, and how you handle your money is the other. Both factors are of equal importance.

Many players, often with justification, lament that they get plenty of winners but fail to benefit from them because their betting is wrong. Yet, they do little to correct this unfortunate situation. Furthermore, since the advent of exotic wagering, this failure to benefit from winners has become an even greater hazard to the bettor's financial well being.

Too often, too many players will use a good-priced key horse in an exacta only to have the key win and the add-on run out. This, along with many other betting errors can only compound losses. Bookkeeping will show just how costly this and other such practices can be. In effect, record-keeping will enable a bettor to quickly learn what he is doing wrong and what he is doing correctly.

The catch is that such record-keeping requires a special kind of courage, or possibly, intestinal fortitude would be the more appropriate phrase. The reason for this is simply human nature. It's a pleasure to make entries on a winning day, but it is psychologically much more difficult to keep one's accounting up-to-date during one of those inevitable losing spells.

But, it becomes a lot easier if you recognize the vast benefits to be derived from following through. As a matter of fact the dry spells can prove a blessing in disguise. Studying them to ascertain their cause can be of immense benefit.

If one were to win with monotonous regularity there would not be much to gain by keeping records. It's the analyzing of our losing bets and the correcting of our errors that enable us to improve.

Aside from the obvious fact that record-keeping will pinpoint wins and losses (which we suspect many players may not wish to recognize), it offers a number of other advantages as well which we'll detail further on.

But, back to our businessman analogy; it would not be conceivable that one could operate for long without maintaining proper books. He wouldn't know where his money is going and where it's coming from. He also wouldn't know what part of the business was profitable and what part was showing losses.

Well, exactly the same situation applies to one's racing activities.

Are you showing profits on your straight bets and losing your shirt with exactas? Are your win bets faring better than your place bets, or vice versa? Are you betting more on losers than on winners? Could it be that you are more skilled with certain types of races than with others? Should your exacta bets be limited to certain field sizes? Do you do great with sprinters and foul up when it comes to routers? Are those "easy" short-field handicaps and stakes costing you money?

Questions such as these and many more can readily be answered with a businesslike form of bookkeeping. They cannot be answered on the basis of guesswork. Record keeping enables a player to learn what type races he should avoid and what type he should concentrate on.

Or, if you don't care to avoid the races that get pin-pointed as weaknesses, at least a recognition of such weakness will hopefully cause a change and an improvement in the approach used.

We previously used the phrase "properly maintained." In other words, we implied that sloppy or half-baked records would do little good. One's record-keeping must be thorough enough to lend itself to detailed analysis.

Setting Up Your Records

The following offers the "bookkeeping" headings or the "set-up" that we have found to be most helpful.

We'll first present the headings and then, where necessary, explain the need for each. In practice these various headings are placed horizontally across the page, but here, due to space limitations, we'll run them vertically.

For the sake of clarity we'll place a make-believe notation alongside each heading. These short-hand notations are similar to the type used in my own record-keeping. You may choose, of course, to use others, and may also choose other headings. However, the headings suggested are the one's your scribe has found to best lend themselves to analysis.

Let me emphasize that symbols and notations go *beneath* the headings.

1-Date & Track Condition	2/2/90 Fst
2-Bet & Type	8-6K XBx
3-Odds/Action	5/2 Up
4-Return	$38.20
5-Result (W&P)	$7.00 3.80
6-Type Race/Fld	6F ANW1 12
7-Trainer-Jockey	Bell / Cordero
8-Last Out & Class	4' S

Line One should be obvious. "Fst" is the abbreviation for a fast track.

Line Two shows that $8.00 was wagered on an exacta box.

The "6K" means that the No. 6 horse was the key horse used. This latter point is important because when it comes time to make a breakdown of your bets you can then determine how you would have fared if you had bet your "strong" horse alone rather than in an exacta. This assumes, of course, that you are selecting a potential winner first and then using it as a key with secondary horses to create a box or boxes.

The reason for including the number six is that I note each bet on my program while at the track so that when I get home and actually record my day's transactions I don't have to guess, I know exactly which horse, how much and what was bet.

Another reason to note if there was a key horse is because occasionally I may box an exacta simply because the race appears to lie between two or three horses and in consequence I have no key horse. Therefore a notation to this effect helps one to analyze the results achieved between the two types of exacta boxes - with a key and without a key.

Furthermore, I save both my program and the Daily Racing Form so that if an occasion arises for me to check back on something, my various notations enable me to know precisely what transpired.

Line Three denotes that the odds on the key horse were 5/2 at post-time, and that it went up (U) in the betting as opposed to having remained the same (S), or having gone down (D) from an early MONEY line. We strongly suggest - again - NOT using the track's morning line.

The morning line, as we've emphasized previously, merely represents one individual's guess (albeit an educated one) as to what the final odds will be. We have no interest in guesses. We're interested in what actually transpires in the mutuel pool itself.

Many players are influenced by how the betting goes. Therefore, by noting the betting action that took place with your selection, you are then in the position of knowing EXACTLY how much or how little you should let the odds influence your selections.

For example: You find that the majority of your losing bets

are horses that went up in the odds (or vice versa). Obviously this knowledge should then serve to guide your actions in the future. BUT, without keeping records you would have no way to know that playing such horses was one of your weaknesses.

Line Four gives the gross return, if any. If you had bet an exacta, and then a horse separately you would require two lines. This is so because you have to be able to differentiate among the returns and results achieved from various type bets. This is the only way to learn which is the preferred approach.

Example:
Race 4: Return (from exacta box) 0.
Race 4. Return (from straight bet) $22.60

Line Five is reserved for the actual mutuel results. In other words, the results for win and place as displayed on the mutuel board. I don't bother with the show hole, but that's just a personal approach. This line would be reserved for both your key horse results, and for the results achieved by whatever straight betting you might have done.

If you had bet $10 to place you still would show the WIN and PLACE mutuel prices. This enables you to see which slot, overall, was most productive. The chances are that if you incline toward chalk you'd find that the place hole was most advantageous. Contrarily if most of your wagering is on horses from 5/1 on up, it's more than likely the win end would prove best.

Line Six defines the distance (6-furlongs) and the type of race conditions that were involved. It also indicates field size.

In our illustration "ANW1" stands for an allowance race conditioned for non-winners (NW) of one race other than a maiden or claimer. If the race had been a claiming race my shorthand might have read, "MC325 M." This would be interpreted to mean a maiden claiming race with a top and bottom tag of $35,000 down to $30,000. My horse was entered at the middle price of $32,500. The "12" is the field size meaning there were 12 betting interests. Stable entries count as one.

The importance of Line Six cannot be over-emphasized. This is the line that will help you most to analyze your handicapping. It will possibly direct your attention to the fact that you do well with route races and do poorly in sprints. Or that you do great with non-claimers but are showing extensive losses when you bet claimers.

Line Seven requires no explanation.

Line Eight shows that the selection ran fourth in its last effort and the "S" (Same) conveys that it had run back today in the same class range as in its last race. A move-up would be indicated with a "U," (Up) and a move-down would be a "D" (Down).

After a number of races have been recorded, one can tell from this last bit of shorthand how he or she fared with drop-downs, move-ups and horses that ran back in similar company. Very important.

This can also be helpful if you cared to see if a difference existed in class drops, or heists between claiming horses and non-claiming horses.

For example: Do horses moving up in class fare better among non-claimers than they do within the claiming ranks?

Well, I trust the foregoing effort has not been wasted and that the reader has been convinced of the importance of record keeping. There is simply no other way that one can ferret out his or her weaknesses. However, if one prefers not to know their handicapping shortcomings that, of course, is a purely personal matter.

The Key Concepts of Winning

This handicapper's philosophy of racing incorporates the belief that in order to win one must know more and have access to more information than one's fellow fans. Just knowing what they know, using the same reference sources they use, and having the same beliefs they have can only mean losing in the same way that most fans lose.

Therefore, if the way followed by most others is not the road to profits, obviously it becomes incumbent on the serious player to seek or create a different approach. My approach has been to first ask a question and then - if the answer was not forthcoming - do whatever work and research was necessary to provide a statistically valid answer.

This is a belief that I've abided by, and worked at, for most of my many years as a racing enthusiast.

The Daily Racing Form is the horseplayer's bible and this is as it should be. The Form contains indispensable information. But, it still is not enough. Supplementary information is required. There is an interesting anecdote that ties in with this thinking, and concerns that perennial folk hero George E. Smith, better known to horseplayers as "Pittsburgh Phil."

Phil, who operated around the turn of the century, is reported by his biographer, Edward W.Cole, to have left a fortune of $1,700,000 to his heirs; all of which is alleged to have been earned from betting on horses. It would appear that Phil's ace-in-the-hole was the fact he created his own past performances long before such cumulative information was made public property. In other words Phil's success was founded on possessing information that other bettors did not have.

In Phil's day, unlike the present, one did play against the house. The house in that instance meant shrewd bookmakers. To beat them consistently one had to be head and shoulders above the crowd.

Currently the problem is tough enough, but nowhere near the degree that applied in Phil's era. In any case, if one is willing to accept Pittsburgh Phil as a role model, the supplementary information offered in the following should serve you well providing you put it to practical use, and apply the knowledge in your day-to-day handicapping.

My Daily Record Sheet

We've reproduced below a one-page sample showing how we maintained a day-by-day record of over 2,300 consecutive races covering a period of approximately 10 months of New York racing. This data is unique inasmuch as it not only required several hours of labor each day, but also necessitated

HOW TO MAINTAIN RECORDS

		FAVORITE						SECOND						THIRD						DATES				
DRT / SAP / TNE / NER	R Fd	odds	d/u/sh/l	n/c	CL	Win	Plce	Odds	d/u/s	H/L	Class	Win	Plce	Odds	d/u/s	H/L	Class	Win	Plce	EX	Trainer-Jock	+/-	Ref	W/O
1																								
2																								
3																								
4																								
5																								
6																								
7																								
8																								
9																								
Gr. Wins	Day Totl						GW	DT						GW	DT									
Gr. Place	Grnd Totl						GP	GT						GP	GT									

daily attendance at the track.

My actual worksheet was 8 1/2 x 11 inches and contained space for two days of racing.

We'll strive to explain each heading, and the reason for it, in crystal clear fashion. In part, the purpose of reproducing this form is to convey to the reader some realization of the tremendous amount of time and effort that went into the project.

In reviewing this data I'm reminded of an observation made by Alexander Pope. Paraphrased, he stated that every hour of synthesis should be accompanied by a year of research. His point is a valid one.

Our procedure will be to first explain each item, and then present the information that was eventually abstracted.

Before going into a detailed explanation of this record, the reader might find an observation to be of interest. The format that you're viewing is by no means what the original layout looked like when this project was first conceived. The original was positively primitive compared to the way the final form shaped up, and contained only about 66% of the information shown herein.

Each sheet contained information relative to 18 individual events i.e., two full days of New York racing.

The Daily Record Sheet Explained

Starting with the top line and working from left to right; The first heading, **"DST,"** stands for distance of race. This should be self-explanatory except perhaps for pointing out that under this heading **"M"** indicates a mile race and **"6"** would indicate a 6-furlong race.

The next heading is **"RAN."** Beneath this we use the symbols **"W"** for with-pace; **"F"** for front-runner, and **"O"** for off-pace. Front-runner explains itself. With-pace means a horse that stayed within 3-1/2 lengths of the pace-setter during the entire running. Off-pace describes a horse that for at least the first quarter mile was more than 3-1/2 lengths off the leader. These symbols describe the running style of the eventual winner of the specific race in question.

In combination with the heading **"DST,"** the purpose of describing the running style of each winner was to help establish which type runner is best favored at which distance.

"TPE" stands for class of race involved. Beneath this you'll note such short-hand symbols as **"3UC," "3UMC," "3UH-1"** and **"3UA1."** The **"3"** indicates age. **"U"** means up, and **"C"** stands for claiming race. Thus **"3UC"** is a race for 3-years-olds and up in a claiming race.

"A1" as you suspected stands for allowance for non-winners of one other than maiden or claimer. **"2A1"** would mean an **A1** allowance for 2-year-olds. **"H"** signifies a handicap race. **"H-1"** therefore indicates a Grade One handicap race. **"MS,"** of course means Maiden Special Weights, and **"MC"** is shorthand for maiden claimer.

None of the symbols have to be clearly understood inasmuch as all pertinent information derived from these records will be presented later in a compact and clear fashion.

However, we feel that an explanation of how the data was originally recorded is necessary in order to give the reader confidence in the conclusions arrived at.

Our major interest was in determining whatever facts we could relative to the top three choices in each race. The very top line should therefore explain itself.

It creates a category for Favorites, Second choices, and Third choices, and shows how they fared in each race. Following these three categories is a heading showing the dates of the 18 races which each sheet evaluated.

Our investigation was confined to the first three choices simply because we feel they are the most logical ones to work and offer the best potential for profit inasmuch as one of the three will be a winner in more than two out of every three races (seven out of every 10 would be more accurate).

Expressing this differently: If we correctly assume that the average field size is composed of a fraction less than nine horses, it means that the top three choices comprise only a third of the contestants, but win more than two-thirds of all the races.

Also, as my pseudonymous friend William L. Scott points out in his innovative book *"Investing At The Racetrack,"* one of these three choices will run second more than 90% of the time. These figures certainly provide fodder for thought and we'll give them considerable attention as we proceed.

We now move down to the second line of headings. Beneath FAVORITE is the letter **"R."** This means race and below it the number of each race is specified. Alongside R we see **"Fd"** which stands for field size and beneath this we've recorded the number of betting units in each race.

Our next heading is **"odds."** This provides the final odds that the favorite went off at in that particular race. Then in the same box you'll note that there's another figure such as 5, 2, etc. This indicates how the favorite finished in its previous race.

Next we note the heading **"d/u/s."** This evaluates the wagering trend. **"d"** means that the horse in question moved down in the odds by post time compared to an acceptable early-money line. No attention was paid to the track's Morning Line for reasons advanced elsewhere in this text.

"U" means the betting trend was up, and **"s"** indicates that the horse's odds remained the same. Example: An early money line showed 5/1, and the final odds were the same (s).

Our next category reads **"h/l"** which stands for high, and low with an **"A"** squeezed in as an abbreviation for average. This shows if the particular choice was high, low or average odds relative to its betting position (favorite, second choice, etc.) and size of field.

In reference to a favorite, the field size provides the only criterion to determine if it went off at relatively high, low or average odds. But in the case of the second and third choices, we regarded their odds as being influenced by two factors; the favorite's odds and the field size.

Our next box contains the symbol **"CL."** which is our abbreviation for Class. A **"D"** indicates a drop in class. **"S"** means it remained within the same class, and **"U"** indicates a class heist. In some instances you'll note another letter such as **T, M,** or **B** is used. This implies that the race was a claiming race and that the horse in question was entered at either the top, bottom or middle price. Example: **"U/M"** would mean that Horse X moved up in claiming value, and was entered for the middle price as opposed to either the top or bottom price.

Assume a claiming horse remained within the same category but was raised in price. For example, in a $12,000 + $14,000 claiming race, Horse A was raised from a previously entered price of $12,000 to today's price of $13,000.

We would show this as follows: S/M and then an arrow pointing upward. This symbolizes that the horse in question remained within the same class but moved up from its previous bottom price to a middle price for the current race. An arrow pointing down would, of course, show that the horse's trainer had taken an opposite action.

The next two boxes read **"Win"** and **"Place."** Beneath these we give the payoffs if any, and necessarily omit the final digit. Example: 5.2 and 3.2 means the horse won and paid $5.20 with the place payoff being $3.20.

We next deal with the **SECOND CHOICE**. The six separate boxes under this heading contain exactly the same information as that given for the favorite. Then, of course, the same applies to the **THIRD CHOICE**.

The first heading in our fourth "info" box under **"DATES,"** reads **"EX."** This stands for Exactas. You'll note the first numbers entered are 25.80 which is what the exacta paid when the second choice won and the favorite ran second. Move to the left for checking purposes and you'll see what the win payoffs were for the two horses in any particualr exacta involving any two of the top three choices. We only recorded payoffs for exacta races that involved two of the first three choices.

Our next sub-head **"Trainer-Jock"** is self-explanatory, except for the fact that this refers to the winner, regardless. In other words, the winner involved was not necessarily one of the top three choices.

Next we note **"+/-."** This tells us if the race was at the same, less or greater distance than the winner's last race. **"S"** was used for same distance. **"L"** indicated a lesser distance, and the plus sign meant added distance. In this instance the information also was not confined to the first three choices. It applied to all winners.

"**Ref**" means Reference, and the numbers below refer to a page number enabling us to check back on a trainer's last winning race in case we sought additional information about him. Example: Did he use the same rider? Did he win first out with a claim last time, too? How many wins did he have?

Our final sub-head on this line reads "**W/C.**" This is very abbreviated and stands for odds of the winner, and its class move. Beneath it we show the odds that the winner went off at, regardless of its betting position. We also indicate if it moved up, down or remained within the same class bracket when scoring the win. All winners were noted here.

We wanted a record of First Time Starters and stable entries, but lacking room, we devised a solution. We used a red pencil and circled all such starters among the top three.

Now go to the box on the extreme right side of the page just below the 9th race. You'll see an elongated box. This area was used to describe what the red circle indicated. Numbers such as 2 or 3 denoted whatever race was involved.

The comment "**Claim**" would refer to a last-out claim which was made, and "**Entry**" would indicate a stable entry. "**FTS**," of course, would indicate a First Time Starter.

All of the spaces that followed simply provide areas wherein we entered cumulative totals of the performances of our top three choices.

26. THE WINNING APPROACH

Most race players are the antithesis of the fabled cold-blooded gambler who never loses his cool. The fact is that the average racing fan is invariably a warm-blooded enthusiast who relishes lots of action and excitement. These elements are probably what attracted him to racing in the first place.

Therefore, to expect such an individual to sit and wait endlessly (as many experts advocate) for "the right betting spot" would be akin to expecting a pussy cat to behave like a guard dog. It is beyond the capability of either specie to comply.

Recognizing this to be so, we'll strive to keep the natural inclinations of most players in mind. Rather than harping on the theme that, "Patience is a virtue," we'll consider a wide a range of betting possibilities and advocate for play as much as prudence and common sense permit.

A Betting Plan for Losers

A good introduction to the betting aspect of racing would be to discuss a mistake which is common among race fans. We're referring to the tendency to bet more on losers than winners. This trend is brought about, in part, by the fact that - regardless of how good a selector one might be - it's inevitable he or she will make more losing bets than winning ones.

This seems to create an atmosphere, psychological and otherwise, wherein the player tends to increase the size of his bets when losing, and to decrease them when winning. Obviously this is the opposite of the way things should be. The cure for correcting this ailment is to devise and apply a means of control. The bugaboo of a 20% nut is difficult enough for a fan to crack without unnecessarily increasing his handicap to an even greater degree by wagering unthinkingly.

Let's look at a hypothetical case to insure that we understand this all-too common problem. John goes to the track with $60.00 in his pocket. He makes a $10.00 bet in the first race. His horse wins at 3/1 and he gets back $40.00. Feeling that this is his lucky day he then makes a $25.00 bet and loses.

However, he's still ahead so he again makes a $25.00 bet. This loses and his bankroll is reduced to $40.00. He grows cautious and takes a $10.00 stab at a longshot. This also loses. John's bankroll has now been deflated to $30.00 and time, along with opportunity, seems to be running out.

Our hero likes the favorite in the next race but figures he can't simply make a straight bet because he won't get enough back if the horse wins at a mere 7/5 odds. In consequence, he assumes an attitude of, "Ah! What the hell," and bets $20.00 of his remaining capital on a 6/1 "possibility" that runs nowhere.

And, inevitably, the logical 7/5 choice wins. John now has only $10.00 left.

He thinks that a 4/1 shot in the race coming up has a good chance, and decides he'll play a $10.00 exacta because, if he made a straight win bet, and the horse won, he still wouldn't be even. This is about the way John's mind works.

He fails to consider that he didn't lose all his money with one bet, so why assume he should recoup all of it with one bet?

Nonetheless, he hooks up his legitimate 4/1 choice with an unlikely longshot that he hopes will get second money. Result; the 4/1 horse wins and the longshot, with considerable effort, staggers in last. John is now broke. He's out $60.00 and sends his weary way home - this despite some pretty good handicapping.

The horses didn't defeat John. He defeated himself.

Let me emphasize that this is not an isolated example. In one form or another it is a scenario that repeats itself hundreds of times every day in the week. Sensible betting contributes as much as sensible selections to one's chance of winning. They are of equal importance and neither should be ignored.

Let's look more closely at John's day at the track. He made six bets. Two of his six legitimate choices won and on a $10.00 flat-bet win basis they would have returned $90.00 as against a total outlay of $60.00. Result: A 50% profit on his investment.

In contrast; John's poor betting habits made him a loser in what should have been a satisfying winning day. The reason for his losses: He bet only $10.00 on his lone winning bet, but averaged $18.00 on each of his five losing bets. Obviously John's losses were due more to poor betting practices than to the track's take and breakage.

About Progressive Betting

We'll come back to John in a moment, but this is as good a place as any to correct a misconception held by many fans. A common belief is that some form of progressive betting (wagering an increased amount after each loser) will eventually produce a profit.

Eventually too the world will end, but we'll not be around to see it. The same applies to "eventually" when related to betting. By the time the eventuality occurs one might well be required to be betting millions, especially if one attempts to practice the primitive concept of doubling up after each loss.

Example:

If one starts with a $1.00 bet and chalks up six consecutive losers his next bet will call for $128.00 being wagered. And - even if we assume that this seventh bet wins - it's highly possible it might pay no more than even money. What does this mean? It means that a total of $255.00 was put at risk in order to win one lone dollar.

However, this is seeing things from the bright side. Let's see what happens to an uninitiated fan who gets what he thinks is an original idea. He knows that favorites win about 33% of all races; that means they average one win out of every three trips.

This is a case where a little knowledge can be a dangerous

thing. Joe Fan overlooks that little word "average" and assumes that if favorites score one time out of every three, it follows that if he bets favorites he can't go too many races without getting a winner.

On this basis he puts a modified (but still steep) progression plan into effect, and after each loss increases his previous bet by 25%. The wind up is that our protagonist quickly becomes divested of not only his shirt, but pants, and shoes as well.

Obviously he was not aware that, on a number of occasions, favorites have been known to go as many as 30 and more consecutive races without producing a single win. This, despite their valid overall record of averaging 33% winners.

Summed up, we're saying to forget about progressive plans unless you are a good enough handicapper to be producing a profit on a flat bet basis. If this is the case progressive play can help.

The simple fact is that progressive wagering will not convert a series of losing selections into winning ones. It will only increase losses. On the other hand, a sensible progression plan can serve to enhance the winnings of any handicapping approach that produces even a modest flat-bet win profit.

A Betting Plan for Winners

Let's now get back to John: How do we suggest that he and all other fans like him should wager? Well, I can't offer a panacea for everybody's wagering ills, but will present an original plan that's effective, and the use of which I've advocated on other occasions. It's not really a progression plan although it is based on a form of progression. However, I regard it more in the light of being an essential control; one that prevents me from committing the sin of betting more on losers than winners.

This plan can be adapted for use on a daily or weekly basis, or can be applied to any series of plays such 10, 20 or one hundred individual wagers. To apply this plan in a practical manner, it is necessary to view each type of bet as having its own individual category.

For example: One series could consist of straight win bets.

Another could be exacta bets, and still a third could be place bets. Regardless, each type should be treated as a separate unit.

Keep in mind that our goal is to bet more on winners than losers, or more precisely, how to avoid betting more on losers than winners. Here's how we proceed. Assume that one starts with a $10 bet. It loses. The next bet cannot be LESS than $10.00, but it can be more.

Okay! We next venture $11.00, and if this loses we obviously have averaged $10.50 on each loser. Thus the minimum that our third bet can be is $11.00. If this should win we've succeeded in our goal of averaging more (regardless of how much more) on our winner than on our losers.

On the other hand, if the third bet also lost we could remain with an $11.00 unit for our fourth bet or we could increase the amount because even another $11.00 wager still would serve the purpose of insuring that we have more riding on a possible winning bet than we had on the losing ones.

Explanation: Up until the fourth bet we wagered a total of $32.00 which breaks down to an average of $10.66 per. Therefore, if we again wager $11.00 we're still within the bounds of our objective

To be sure that you understand this approach, let's create another series of possible wagers. $10.00 is bet and the horse wins. Next bet? It could be either the same amount or less. *It could not be more* because if the next bet lost we would have defeated our purpose and wagered more on a loser than on our winner.

Actually, in a case such as this, where the first bet of an intended series wins, it's advisable to simply start a new series. Otherwise the plan becomes too restrictive.

Our second bet (actually the first of a new series) is again $10.00 and it loses. Our new second bet can now be either the same amount ($10.00) or more, but cannot be less. We decide on $12.00, and it also loses. At this point take a minute to note for yourself how much was averaged on the two losing bets.

Obviously the answer is $11.00. This limits us to the option of wagering either $11.00 or more; preferably more, but certainly not less.

Assume that we're suddenly imbued with derring-do and decide on a $14.00 wager that wins. We've then averaged $11.00 on losers and $14.00 on our lone winner. This means we can next make a bet of anywhere from $9.00 on up. Why? Because if we bet $9.00 and lose we've succeeded in lowering our losing average to $10.33, yet still maintained a win average of $14.00.

What happens though if the $9.00 bet wins? We still would be achieving our purpose. We would have maintained the $11.00 average for losers, but our two winners would now average $11.50 per.

Risking the accusation of redundancy; keep in mind that the only object of this plan is to insure that you don't defeat yourself by adding unnecessarily to the normal hazards of race play that confront all fans. When you employ this technique your wagering will be under control at all times.

As a point of interest; our personal experience is that this extremely mild form of progressive wagering results in creating a positive difference of approximately 1-1/2% overall. This means that this betting approach tends to enhance profits (or decrease losses) to that extent.

In conclusion, I thank you for bearing with me, and trust that my efforts will be helpful in making you successful at the tracks!

27. GLOSSARY

Alive - A horse that's obviously being bet in the mutuel pool.

Allowance Races - Race for horses not eligible to be claimed.

Average Favorite - A favorite whose odds range around 8/5.

Being in Jail - A 30-day penalty imposed after a horse is claimed.

Bet Down - A horse whose odds drop.

Board Horses - Usually implies an obviously bet down horse(s).

Booting - Riding - a jockey *boots* a horse home.

Box - The combining of one or more horses with a single bet.

Breakeage - The odd pennies that the track keeps from the payout.

Bug - A term to denote a one, two and three *bug* apprentice allowance.

Bug Boy - An apprentice who gets a weight allowance to compensate for his inexperience.

Bullet - Indicates a fast workout as shown in the Daily Racing form.

Change Leads - Changing from leading with the right leg to the left leg going around a turn.

Claiming Horse -A horse which is eligible to be bought out of a race.

Class - A relative term that implies one horse is superior to another.

Condition Book - The book that trainers use as a guide for placing their horses.

Created Favorite - Not the original betting favorite.

Daily Double - A bet combining winners in two specified races.

Drop-Down - A horse moving down in class or claiming price.

Dutch Book - An attempt to play several horses in such manner that regardless of which wins, a profit is forthcoming.

Exacta - Selecting horses in the same race to run one-two in that order.

Favorite - The horse with the most money wagered on it in the win pool.

Flat Box - Just two horses combined, as opposed to three or more.

Form - Physical condition.

Front Runner - A horse that runs in front.

Guts - A strong competitive spirit.

Haltered - Claimed.

Halterman - One who claims horses.

Heavy Hitters - Big money bettors.

Key - The horse in a parlay or box that you regard as your strong one.

L & A Favorites - Low-priced and average-priced favorites.

Low Favorite - A favorite below the 8/5, the average price.

Low-Priced - See above.

Maiden Claiming Race - A race for non-winners who are eligible to be claimed.

Maiden Race -A race for horses that have never won.

Maiden Special Weights - Maiden races for horses not eligible to be claimed.

Morning Line - A track employee's guess as to how the public will bet.

Natural Favorite - The original favorite in the betting.

Nut - The tax on betting levied by the state and track.

Off-Track - Not fast - muddy, sloppy, holding, binding or soft.

Overbet - A horse with more money wagered on it than it appears to merit.

Overlaid - A horse competing at higher odds than it appears to merit.

Parlay - Betting the total returns from one race on to another.

Play Down - A horse that's bet down in the mutuels.

Racing Conditions - The physical conditions involved in a race.

Route Performance - How a horse performs at a distance beyond a mile.

Router - A horse with demonstrated ability to negotiate a route distance.

Scale of Weights - A universal yardstick for gauging the normal weight to be carried relative to age, sex and distance of race.

Short Field - Seven or fewer horses.

Sprinter - A horse that shows a preference for short distances.

Stable Entry - Two or more horses in same race whose owners share financial interests.

Stake Race - Usually a high type race with rigid specifications for eligibility.

Stiff - A horse obviously not too capable.

Straight - A straight bet means to bet on the win end.

Strings - Means giving the ticket seller a long list of bets.

Three Bug - An apprentice with the maximum allowance of 10 pounds.

Top and Bottom Race - A claiming race offering a graduated claiming price. Example: $14,000 down to $12,000.

Tote Board - The totalisator infield board at the track that shows the money wagered and the resulting odds.

Track Secretary-Handicapper - The individual who dictates what the race conditions will be for any specific meeting.

Trip Handicapping - Looking for mishaps in a previous race that may have prevented a horse from doing its best.

Two Bug - An apprentice who gets a seven pound allowance from the assigned weight.

MASTER GREYHOUND STRATEGY
Prof. Jones' Winning Strategy for Non-Computer Users

THE ULTIMATE WINNING STRATEGY

Finally, the **ultimate advanced winning strategy** that gives serious players the extra edge to **greatly increase** their winning percentages at the track! Regardless of experience or ability, this **essential** strategy package is a **must** for greyhound handicappers intent on **winning**!

BEAT ANY DOG TRACK!

For the **first time** anywhere, Prof. Jones, the world's leading designer of winning software strategies **reveals** his **computer-proven** winning secrets. Developed at a cost of **more than $30,000**, these strategies are now available to you at a fraction of the cost! And best of all, you don't need a computer to learn how to pick **winners after winners** using these **scientific strategies**.

ADVANCED STRATEGIES

You'll learn the latest in advanced winning strategies. Learn how to use **Sloped Speed** and **Advanced Earning Analysis**, the strategies **pros** use to get the **winning** edge, and how to combine them with the strategies in *Winners Guide to Greyhound Betting* for a **powerful edge**. You'll learn how to really determine a greyhound's recent form and **turn that knowledge into cash**.

MORE FEATURES

You'll also receive additional **wheeling systems** to best pick the likely winners and **increase profit expectations** at less cost! The **Expanded Score Chart**, a Prof. Jones **exclusive**, organizes all of the strategies into an easy-to-manage format.

BONUS

The $15 tip sheets, *Insiders' Winning Tips for Greyhound Profit Players*, is included free, and shows you the 10 most important rules for winning at the track. Culled from the top professionals in the business, these hard-to-find tips, put together in one place for the first time, are must-knowledge for the aspiring pro.

To order, send $49.95 plus postage and handling by check or money order to:
Cardoza Publishing, P.O. Box 1500, Cooper Station, New York, NY 10276

THOROUGHBRED HORSERACING LEVEL V™

Prof. Jones Winning Software - For Professional Players

IBM & Compatibles Only - Hard Drive Required

• THE ULTIMATE WINNING PACKAGE!!! •

Groups of questions can be assigned to create your own scores and comparison charts. For example, if you feel 1/2 to final call is "Closing Ability", you can apply only this variable; or you can add lengths gained or lost from stretch to finish.

You truly create your own program from the ground up.

ASSIGN GROUPS			
GROUP	LOW	HIGH	STATUS
JOCKEY TODAY	0	1	OFF
JOCKEY CHANGE	-10	10	ON
EARNINGS	-6	10	ON
TRAINER	0	5	ON
EARLY SPEED	-8	20	ON
1ST CALL	-1	13	OFF
2ND CALL	04	12	ON
FINISH	-1	4	ON
CLOSING	0	5	ON
POST CHANGE	0	3	ON
CLASS CHANGE	0	2	ON
SPEED	-5	6	ON
TOP 3 @ 2 CALL	-4	8	OFF
FITNESS	-6	9	ON
LAST DIST	-0	1	ON
LAST TRACK	02	12	ON

Level V allows Linear Multiple Regression (Artifical Intelligence) to be applied to both your STANDARD VALUES and DATABASE VALUES. The more you run the program, the higher your win percentage will be.

Artifical Intelligence will even tell you if your weighting systems are correct or if they should be changed. You can now create "perfect" weights.

		USING STANDARD SCORES	
NAME	PROJ	MUs	COMPARISONS
4-IRON JOE	1-4	-	1-Concensus
7-CHEF	5-1	↓	3-1/4, 1-Class, 3-Early SP
1-ORPHAN JONES	5-1	↓	1-Post, 3-1/2
5-DEAD HEAT	7-1	2	2-Concensus
9-NOBEL BET	8-1	↓	3-Concensus
2-IMA PRINCE	23-1	↓	2-Post, 1-1/2, 1-Finish
8-NEVER CAUTIOUS	39-1	4	2-Class
3-PRO FOR SURE	42-1	1	
6-NIGHT ROVER	79-1	-	1-Close

- NO MOVE UP
↓ MOVED DOWN
MOVED UP # OF PLACES

NAME	MOVE-UPS
8-NEVER CAUTIOUS	4
5-DEAD HEAT	2
3-PRO FOR SURE	1

Move ups compare standard and any other set of results.

Top 3 in each catagory taken directly from the comparison chart.

Using Standard Scores	
NAME	POINTS
9-NOBEL BET	16
5-DEAD HEAT	15
1-ORPHAN JONES	13
7-CHEF	13
4-IRON JOE	2

'Top Overlays' compares morning line odds and the projected odds.

New advanced betting analysis allows you to program all forms of bets. Complete odds projections are given for each animal and all 'overlays' are displayed.

SUPERFECTA

4	1-5-7-9
1-5-7-9	4
1-5-7-9	1-5-7-9
1-5-7-9	1-5-7-9

4-IRON JOE 7-CHEF 1-ORPHAN JONES
5-DEAD HEAT 9-NOBEL BET

COST IS 24 UNITS

07/03/1990 BOI	RACE NUMBER											
BET TYPE		1	2	3	4	5	6	7	8	9	0	1 1
Win/Place/Show												
Top 2 Any Order	X											
Top 2 Any Order												
Top 3 Any Order	X											
Top 4 Any Order	◆											

Control Keys	
↑ Cursor Up	X Selected
↓ Cursor Down	
→ Cursor Right	◆ Cursor
← Cursor Left	
C -Clear All	▮ Can't Bet
R -Select All	
bets for a race	
V -View a Bet	
<ESC> Exit	

The advanced 'Horse Watch List' links directly to the enter section so animals in trouble last out are flagged instantly.

Race 01	Post 01
Race 02	Post 02
Race 03	Post 03
Race 04	Post 04
Race 05	Post 05
Race 06	Post 06
Race 07	Post 07
Race 08	Post 08
Race 09	Post 09

DISTANCE: 12 WEIGHTING: Route RACE DATE: 06/18/90
HORSE'S NAME: ORPHAN JONES

WATCH LIST
ENTRY DATE: 06/02/90
MESSAGE:
STUMBLED IN FIRST TURN
BUT RECOVERED WELL
PRESS ANY KEY

Create your own Thoroughbred racing program for your track with the first "User Programmable" handicapping product.

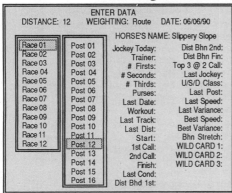

ENTER DATA

DISTANCE: 12   WEIGHTING: Route   DATE: 06/06/90

HORSE'S NAME: Slippery Slope

Race 01	Post 01
Race 02	Post 02
Race 03	Post 03
Race 04	Post 04
Race 05	Post 05
Race 06	Post 06
Race 07	Post 07
Race 08	Post 08
Race 09	Post 09
Race 10	Post 10
Race 11	Post 11
Race 12	Post 12
	Post 13
	Post 14
	Post 15
	Post 16

Jockey Today: Dist Bhn 2nd:
Trainer: Dist Bhn Fin:
Firsts: Top 3 @ 2 Call:
Seconds: Last Jockey:
Thirds: U/S/D Class:
Purses: Last Post:
Last Date: Last Speed:
Workout: Last Variance:
Last Track: Best Speed:
Last Dist: Best Variance:
Start: Bhn Stretch:
1st Call: WILD CARD 1:
2nd Call: WILD CARD 2:
Finish: WILD CARD 3:
Last Cond:
Dist Bhd 1st:

First create the Enter Section that fits your racing philosophy by using questions from the standard system or create your own questions. Questions can be added, deleted, and the order can be changed.

SET TODAYS RACES

DATE: 5/22/1990   TRACK: ALA   # OF RACES 12

RACE	DISTANCE	WEIGHTING	RACE
Race 01	12	Route	Race 09
Race 02	4	Sprint	Race 10
Race 03	7	--------	Race 11
Race 04	0	--------	Race 12
Race 05	0	--------	
Race 06	0	--------	
Race 07	0	--------	
Race 08	0	--------	

Now decide how much weight you desire for each question to be worth in the final score. You control the weighting system rather than wonder what makes the program work.

AVAILABLE WEIGHTING SYSTEMS: 3

Sprint	Standard Weighting File for Sprint races
Route	Standard Weighting File for Route races
Maiden	Standard Weighting File for Maiden races

POST 1 69%
POST 2 65%
POST 3 61%
POST 4 55%
POST 5 43%
POST 6 40%
POST 7 50%
POST 8 67%
POST 9 49%
POST 10 71%
POST 11 41%
POST 12 39%
POST 13 37%
POST 14 39%
POST 15 64%

FIRST   DOWN HILL HARRY
SECOND   ORPHAN JONES
THIRD   NEVER CAUTIOUS

GROUP

JOCKEY TODAY
JOCKEY CHANG
TRAINER
1ST CALL
2ND CALL
FINAL CALL
CLASS CHANGE
POST CHANGE
FITNESS
EARNINGS
CLOSING
SPEED
STRTCH CLOSE
WILD CARD

OVERALL SCORES

PST	NAME	SCORE
10	DOWN HILL HARRY	71
01	ORPHAN JONES	69
08	NEVER CAUTIOUS	67
02	IMA PRINCE	65
15	CITY HALL	64
03	PRO FOR SURE	61
16	MISS BERTHA	58
04	IRON JOE	55
07	CHEF	50
09	NOBEL BET	49
05	DEAD HEAT	43
11	STONE TREASURE	41
06	NIGHT ROVER	40
12	SLIPPERY SLOPE	39
14	JETSDREAM	38

GROUP SCORE

PST	NAME	SCORE
13	SPANKY BOY	85
01	ORPHAN JONES	84
05	DEAD HEAT	79
15	CITY HALL	76
02	IMA PRINCE	69
04	IRON JOE	67
07	CHEF	65
16	MISS BERTHA	61
08	NEVER CAUTIOUS	60
09	NOBEL BET	59
11	STONE TREASURE	58
06	NIGHT ROVER	56
14	JETSDREAM	55
12	SLIPPERY SLOPE	54
03	PRO FOR SURE	53

Level V allows you to keep a database of the last 10 races of each animal at the track. It even allows you to program your own parameters regarding which races are utilized. It also uses total 'Key Memory' so typing is kept to a minimum.

To order, send $799.95 plus postage and handling by check or money order to:
Cardoza Publishing, P.O. Box 1500, Cooper Station, New York, NY 10276